UNSHAKABLE

"They gave me an 85% death sentence.
God gave me a 100% promise of life."

CATHERINE OGIE

Foreword by Apostle Diana Lookabough

This is a work of nonfiction. Some names and identifying details have been changed to protect the privacy of individuals.

For resources and permissions, visit www.NewHeartPublishing.com.

For speaking engagements, bulk orders, and author inquiries, please contact us through the website above.

DISCLAIMER

The content within this book, Unshakable, is for informational and inspirational purposes only and is not intended to replace medical, psychological, legal, or other professional advice. The author shares personal experiences, spiritual reflections, and insights intended to encourage and uplift readers on their journey of faith and healing.

While every effort has been made to represent the experiences and outcomes accurately as described, individual results may vary. Readers are encouraged to consult qualified healthcare professionals before making any decisions regarding their health or treatment.

The author, Catherine Ogie, and NewHeart Publishing disclaim any liability for injury, loss, or damage incurred directly or indirectly by use of the information provided in this book.

Published by NewHeart Publishing

An imprint of Rockhaven Group LLC

ISBN: 978-1-971368-00-9

Printed in the United States of America

Foreword written by Apostle Diana Lookabough

ENDORSEMENTS

"A beautifully written book that is engaging, thoughtful, clear, and compelling from start to finish. This book is a masterful and compassionate guide to healing, health, and true wholeness. Written with clarity, wisdom, and deep understanding, it bridges lived experience, profound insight, and practicality in a way that feels authentic, grounding, and transformative. Cathy does more than inform through her story; she invites the reader into a journey of restoration that honors the soul, body, and spirit as an integrated whole. What makes this book particularly exceptional is its balance of depth and accessibility. Complex truths are conveyed with grace, yet every page serves as a call to empower readers toward lasting well-being. It is not merely a book to be read and tucked away, but one to be lived—offering hope, direction, and practical tools for real-life transformation. In a world where many are struggling with disease, hopelessness, and weariness, this is a timely contribution to the conversation on healing, health, and holistic well-being. Anyone seeking renewal, clarity, and a deeper sense of wholeness in body, soul, or spirit will find this book to be a trusted companion, a comforting guide, and a source of inspiration. I wholeheartedly recommend it."

—DR. DAMILOLA BABANJI, DO, DipABLM Board
Certified in Internal Medicine and Lifestyle Medicine

TESTIMONIALS

"While reading Catherine's recounting of God's unseen hand bringing people into her life, I was reminded of how God brought Catherine into my own life as proof that He truly cares. Knowing that she is a woman with an intimate knowledge of God gives the prayers and strategies she shares exceptional weight and credibility. Unshakable is a compelling narrative that testifies to the reality of God—His power, faithfulness, and unfailing love. Keep this book close, because when the fires of life inevitably come, you will need these strategies to survive without even smelling like smoke."

—Josiane Joseph, MD, PhD
Founder, Double Doc J LLC
Hollywood, Florida, USA

"Forget survival stories. This is a resurrected life, delivered with medical-grade proof that miracles still happen. If you need unshakeable evidence that you are never too far gone, read this book."

— Rose Adamu, Christian Association of Nigeria, Lagos

"Catherine's journey is a tender tapestry woven with threads of divine encounters, each one a whisper of God's relentless pursuit of our hearts.

As I turned the pages, I found myself wrapped in the warmth of a love that's both personal and profound—a reminder that God crafts connections with precision, bringing people into our lives like whispered promises.

Her story isn't just a narrative; it's a testament to a love that seeks, finds, and anchors us in the messiest of moments.

Unshakable is a gentle shelter, a place to breathe, grieve, and rediscover the heartbeat of faith. It's a reminder that even in life's rawest fires, God's love isn't just a shield—it's the fragrance that makes the flames dance differently."

—DR. SHAKA OVIE ERNEST, PhD
Founder, Dela Leverage
Malta, Europe

"The core of this testimony is the unyielding character of the Healer. This book is an encounter with the One who walks into ICU rooms and whispers, 'You will live and not die.' No diagnosis can override divine destiny."

— Sylvia, Dallas, TX

"When I received my own heart diagnosis, I remembered Catherine's story—15% chance of survival. I chose to believe for 100% victory. Six months later, I'm medication-free and thriving. This book saved my life."

— Flora Nwachukwu, Educator, UK

"Catherine Ogie has written more than a testimony; she's crafted a masterpiece of faith. Unshakable proves that God still moves mountains and heals the broken."

— Apostle Niyi Aniyah, Lead Pastor,
Waterbrook's International Church

"Unshakable is dynamite in the hands of anyone who dares to believe in miracles. Cathy's implicit trust in God never wavered. This book will kindle the fire of faith in weary hearts."

— Oguazi Onyemobi, President,
Jesus Power Outreach Ministries, Chicago, USA

"Get ready to embark on a journey of inspiration and hope as you delve into the pages of Unshakable. Cathy's unfiltered and sincere narrative of her life-altering medical crisis will not only bolster your faith in God but also equip you with the resilience to stand strong when life's pillars are shaken."

— Rev. Joe Egbe, Good News Outreach, UK

"I felt seen on every page. Unshakable is a brave, nakedly honest conversation with the person battling in silence, showing how faith took the mic and silenced the fear. A stunning read."

— Pauline, Grateful Reader, UK

"Prepare to be uplifted and empowered as you read Cathy's chapter on 'Weapons of Warfare.' Her profound insights revolutionized my prayer life, and I believe they can do the same for you. The depression that had haunted me for years was completely shattered."

— Nicole Kayunga, Minnesota, USA

"The chapter on intimacy with the Father broke me open in the best way. Cathy's transparency transformed my walk from religious duty to deep love. I keep copies of Unshakable in our family waiting room. Faith and medicine can work together beautifully."

— Julie O Shaka, Patlian School, Ontario, Canada

"When I felt God had abandoned me while battling my health issues, Catherine's words in the 'Via Dolorosa' chapter reminded me that Jesus walks the way of suffering with us. Unshakable has the power to restore faith and hope, even in the darkest of times."

— Lawrence Michael, Birmingham, United Kingdom

"UNSHAKEABLE by Catherine Ogie is more than a book—it's a holy encounter. Catherine doesn't just share what God did; she reveals how He carried her through, using forgiveness, worship, and community as instruments of healing and strength. Writing as a single mother fighting for her life, she points not to herself, to God, who met her in surrender with both healing and purpose. This powerful testimony reminds us that miracles still happen,

God's report overrides man's, and faith can rise even when strength is gone."

—Sandra Wickham, A Woman of Faith
Who Believes Deeply in the Power of Testimony,
Healing, and God's Promises, Plano, TX

"Countless hours have been put into this book. Tears and effort and frustration and love. If you're reading this, then it's worth it."

— Princess Ogie

DEDICATIONS

Author's Note and Dedication

To Abba Father

Abba Father, the Author of my story, the Healer of my heart, and the Keeper of my soul.

This book is Yours. Every page, every tear, every miracle.

You saw me drowning in weakness, and You raised me with resurrection power. When doctors gave me statistics, You gave me promises. When the enemy whispered death, You declared life.

You are the One who called me by a new name—Newheart. I will never stop testifying to Your goodness.

You wrapped me in peace when fear tried to suffocate me. You surrounded me with angels when I could barely breathe. You spoke healing when everything in the natural screamed otherwise—a transformative miracle that still fills me with awe and encourages others to trust in Your power.

"I shall not die, but live, and declare the works of the Lord." (Psalm 118:17)

And that is what this is. A declaration. A testimony. A love letter back to You.

You were not only my Deliverer; You were my Comforter. You walked me through fire and refined me—not to destroy me, but to reveal Your glory in me.

You are Jehovah Rapha, my Healer. El Roi, the God who sees me. And El Shaddai, the Almighty, who sustained me when my strength was gone.

This is for Your glory. This is my complete surrender and acceptance of Your will and plan for my life.

This is the oil from the crushing, the blessing that comes from enduring trials in faith.

And as long as I have breath, I will proclaim: You are faithful. I pray this encourages you to believe in His unwavering faithfulness, even in your darkest moments.

For My Mama and Papa Now Rejoicing in Heaven

To my Mama, a relentless intercessor, your prayers crossed oceans and continue to uplift me. When I was a 19-year-old girl dreaming of America, you laid your hands on that dream and asked God for favor. I feel your prayers working in my life, reminding me that Heaven's support is never silent.

Though your chair at the table is empty, your torch of prayer still burns over me and over Princess. You passed the mantle of intercession to me as you crossed over, and I wear it now as a daughter and as a mother.

To my Papa, who cheered for me long before the world knew my name, and to you, Mama, whose prayers echo in every open door and every deliverance—this book is part of your harvest. I lay it at your feet with gratitude and honor.

Dedication to My Daughter

For my daughter, Ebunoluwa—Princess, my anchor, my joy, my miracle.

In the darkest hours, when my body was too weak to stand and my spirit was nearly crushed, you stood in the gap for me. You prayed when I could not. You whispered words of hope when I could not find them myself. You took care of me with a strength that defied your years and a love that only a daughter can give.

You became not just my daughter, but my caregiver, my confidant, and my closest friend. In every hospital visit, every tear-soaked night, every whispered prayer—you were there. You carried me in ways no medicine or machine could ever replicate.

Your belief when I was too broken to believe. Your love when I felt unlovable. Your care when I was at my weakest—these were the true healers. You called me back to life.

This book is for you, Ebunoluwa. May it remind you that you are seen by Heaven and deeply loved by me. May every chapter echo with the truth that your faith, your love, and your unshakable hope have been a testament to the power of God's goodness amid suffering.

My beautiful Ebunoluwa, a gift from God. May you always know that you are the legacy of His healing and the promise of His faithfulness.

Author's Note and Dedication

To Abba Father

Abba Father, the Author of my story, the Healer of my heart, and the Keeper of my soul.

This book is Yours. Every page, every tear, every miracle.

You saw me drowning in weakness, and You raised me with resurrection power. When doctors gave me statistics, You gave me promises. When the enemy whispered death, You declared life.

You are the One who called me by a new name—Newheart. I will never stop testifying to Your goodness.

You wrapped me in peace when fear tried to suffocate me. You surrounded me with angels when I could barely breathe. You spoke healing when everything in the natural screamed otherwise—a transformative miracle that still fills me with awe and encourages others to trust in Your power.

"I shall not die, but live, and declare the works of the Lord."
~ Psalm 118:17 ~

Dedication to My Mama and Papa in Heaven

To my Mama, a relentless intercessor, your prayers crossed oceans and continue to uplift me. When I was a 19 year old girl dreaming of America, you laid your hands on that dream and asked God for them, I feel your prayers working in my life, reminding me that Heaven's support is never silent.

Though your chair at the table is empty, your torch of prayer still burns over me and over Princess. You passed the mantle of intercession to us ie you crossed over, and I wear it now as a daughter, and as a mother.

Dedication to My Daughter

For my daughter, Ebunoluwa—Princess, my anchor, my joy, my miracle.

In the darkest hours, when my body was soe week to stand and my spirit was neatly craecls, crushed, you tould in the gap for weu enegangrd when I caudd me. You cerages sot n reehon sands on. You toke care as the with a smught that deifed your yeurs me and a bov that only g ourgese so ...

You became not just my daughter, but my caregine, my costidant, and my clowes mortd. In every. Et gims ther other fies easted right euery echoes me prayer, qfil teanclons. You raitied no it way: por reedlows or mithow could owr nakl.ate. You doldy when I not no praken to boalave. Last neur when I havel freen the strieues in woue nackess montiens.

My beautitial Ebunohwa, a gift from God. May you always know that you are the ligocy of Fils healing and the promise of His falitifchess.

With Deepest Gratitude to the One Reading This

Perhaps you've just received a diagnosis. Maybe your body feels like it's betraying you, and you've whispered, "God, where are You?"

I've been where you are. And I want you to know—this book is for you, in this moment of your life.

You are not forgotten. You are not alone. You are not too far gone.

The same Jesus who wept at the tomb, who touched lepers, who stood in the fire with Shadrach, Meshach, and Abednego— He is with you now. His comforting presence surrounds you, and He will never leave your side.

You may feel pressed, but you will not be crushed. You may be walking through the fire, but you will not be burned.

He is still the God who heals. Healing is not just what He does—it's who He is.

To the Medical Teams Who Showed Up with Knowledge and Compassion

You became the hands of God when I couldn't lift my own. Your compassion and patience in treatment reminded me that your work restores hope and life, and I am grateful for your dedication.

I saw angels—and they wore scrubs.

Your calling is holy. You don't just extend life; you restore hope. This book bears your fingerprints, too.

To Every Intercessor, Prayer Warrior, and Watchman Who Cried Out on My behalf

You formed a hedge of protection when I was too weak to pray. Your midnight prayers reached Heaven. Your texts, voice notes, and silent support—it all mattered.

The miracles I experienced didn't come from medicine alone. They came from your persistent faith. From the promise that:

"The effectual fervent prayer of the righteous availeth much." (James 5:16)

If you're reading this, may this dedication whisper truth into your soul:

Healing is possible. Wholeness is promised. And you are deeply loved—not only by those who surround you, but by the God who has never left your side and never will.

You are not just a patient. You are a beloved child of God, and your worth is immeasurable.

EPIGRAPH

"Beyond the shadow of an 85% medical sentence, lies God's unbroken 100% life."

— Catherine Ogie

FOREWORD

Catherine has penned an inspiring account of her miraculous healing and profound faith journey. This book is a testament to Faith, Trust, Prayer, Determination, and Divine Persistence. Prepare to be moved, and I encourage you to share this powerful story

For years, I've had the privilege of knowing Catherine through our Women's House of Zion ministry. I've witnessed firsthand her unwavering faith and remarkable courage as she navigated this incredible journey. When faced with a grim 15% chance of survival, Catherine chose to stand firm in her belief in a God of 100% victory.

What elevates this testimony beyond the extraordinary healing itself—though that alone is remarkable—is the intimate, honest way Catherine invites us into her struggle. She doesn't shy away from revealing moments of doubt, the internal battles with fear, or the complex challenges of balancing faith with medical realities. Her genuine vulnerability amplifies the splendor of her triumph.

This book transcends being merely a testimony; it serves as a guiding map for anyone confronting seemingly impossible circumstances. Catherine generously shares practical strategies, potent Healing Scriptures, and clear, step-by-step guidance for spiritual warfare. She beautifully illustrates that healing is not solely about recovery, but about embracing the person God destined you to be.

I am confident that God will use Catherine's narrative to ignite faith in countless hearts. Her transformative journey, from "Catherine" to "Catherine Newheart," stands as a powerful reminder that our God continues to rewrite destinies, and that no medical prognosis holds ultimate authority when Heaven has the final decree.

—Diana Lookabaugh

Apostle for Women's Houses of Zion

Glory of Zion International

TABLE OF CONTENTS

INTRODUCTION

No bypass, no stent—just a countdown. They said I had only a 15% chance of living. My body, riddled with inflammation, blood clots, and heart failure, was shutting down. I wore a heart defibrillator because the doctors feared my heart would stop at any moment. At night, I whispered my prayers through shallow breaths, wondering if I'd wake up. I wasn't just battling sickness—I was facing a storm that came to silence my purpose. But through faith, I found hope that kept me fighting.

But storms don't have the final say.

This book is not a survival story. It's a resurrection. It's the fireproof evidence that God still heals, that miracles still happen, and that no diagnosis can override divine destiny. I was once frail, voiceless, and close to death—but God breathed life into me again, transforming me into a living testament of His power and grace. I understand you may wonder if divine healing is real or possible for you. My experience aims to inspire trust that divine intervention is not just possible but accessible through faith, even in the darkest moments.

Unshakable is the testimony of what happens when faith takes the mic and fear is forced to sit down. I questioned many times if

God's promises were real during my darkest hours. I prayed when my hands trembled and declared when my voice quivered, and when my legs could no longer hold me. It's about healing—yes—but more than that, it's about the Healer. The One who walks through ICU rooms and wilderness valleys, whispering, "You will live and not die," even when doubt tried to creep in.

I am deeply grateful for Apostle Diana Lookabough, whose prayers, wisdom, and spiritual covering steadied me during some of the most difficult moments of this journey. Her words in the foreword beautifully capture what God was doing behind the scenes, even when I could not see it.

You're not just a reader; you're a vital part of this journey. Every chapter is filled with Scripture, soaked in prayer, and strengthened by raw honesty. Whether you're in a hospital room, grieving a diagnosis, battling mental exhaustion, or standing in the gap for someone else, your presence in these pages was anticipated and is deeply valued. Your resilience and faith are powerful, and this story is a testament to that strength.

Inside these pages, you'll walk with me through the fire and watch how God mantled me in gold.

God gave me a new heart, literally and spiritually. And He told me to take pictures because people would never believe the transformation unless they saw it for themselves. Well, here it is—in full color, raw truth, and divine wonder. This is a testament to God's miraculous power that can transform even the impossible into reality.

I'll share not only my miraculous recovery but also the spiritual principles and divine strategies that God gave me through dreams, scriptures, and encounters. These include practical steps like forgiveness--letting go of resentment, worship-praising through pain, and community support leaning on others. These tools can help you unlock your own healing. I'll show you how forgiveness unlocked my healing, how worship became my medicine, and how the power of community carried me so you can apply these principles in your own journey of faith and recovery.

I was neither a pastor nor a theologian. I was a single mother, a servant of God, fighting for her own life. I didn't just get better. I got bolder. I didn't just find peace. I found purpose. I didn't just recover—I was made brand new.

The Stakes: On June 18th, 2023—Father's Day—I was told I wasn't a good candidate for bypass surgery. I had suffered a silent heart attack. My ejection fraction was so low, just 9 to 12 percent, that the doctors said I only had a 15% chance of survival. Blood clots were in my heart, liver, and lungs. My esophagus was thinning. My kidneys were inflamed. I had edema, IBS, and diabetes. My body was shutting down. They sent me home to prepare for the worst.

Have you ever been told it's over—your life, your health, your destiny?

This is **UNSHAKABLE:**

How I Survived the Death Sentence, Found Radical Faith, and Rose with a New Heart.

CHAPTER 1

CALL ME NEWHEART

―――――❧―――――

The Day Heaven Rewrote My Name

Some stories begin with a crisis; this one begins with a divine interruption that refused to let me quietly disappear.

A few weeks before a long-awaited vacation I had planned, my body began resisting every remedy I trusted. What started as a persistent cold refused to break. My usual go-to—a hot tea with ginger, cloves, lemon, and cayenne pepper—offered no relief, and even after a visit to urgent care, the symptoms returned stronger than before.

I had already canceled a speaking engagement, yet I was determined to keep the trip on the calendar. I reminded myself of a truth I had lived by for years: "The Lord will perfect that which concerns me" (Psalm 138:8, NKJV)—believing God would meet me even in my weariness. I wasn't only craving rest for myself; I wanted my teenage daughter, Princess, to come with me so we could step away from the relentless pace of school, work, and responsibility. I was holding onto the hope of uninterrupted mother-daughter time—a quiet, sacred reset—before life demanded everything from us again.

As the days passed, I tried to maintain my normal rhythm. I went to work, wrapped up loose ends, and told myself that once the vacation began, my body would finally catch up with my intentions. I had pushed through discomfort before, and I believed I could do it again.

On Tuesday evening, I stayed late at the office to prepare for my upcoming time away. My supervisor, Cora—an unwavering source of support—noticed immediately that something was off. Later that night, she called to check on me. "Ms. Cathy," she said gently, "maybe you should see a doctor before your flight. You don't look well." I thanked her for her concern but assured her I would be fine. The next day, she wished me safe travels for my Friday night flight, and I took her words as confirmation that everything was still moving forward.

By Friday morning, my body told a different story. I woke up completely drained. Every joint ached, and my ankles were so swollen I could barely walk. Still, I tried to reason with myself. Maybe I was just overtired. Maybe rest was all I needed. But the symptoms were no longer something I could explain away. With growing clarity and reluctance, I decided to cancel my flight. Letting go of the vacation felt heavier than disappointment—it felt like admitting that something was truly wrong. but it was a step in trusting God's perfect timing and guidance, which strengthened my faith in His plan.

For over two decades, I had dedicated myself to serving others—teaching, mentoring, coaching, and interceding for the broken. I gave out of overflow, and sometimes from empty. I was the strong one. A woman of faith. A daughter of hope. Until one day, I was not.

The next day, Saturday, October 15, 2022, I experienced a brief sense of relief. Hoping the worst had passed, Princess and I went out to lunch. For a moment, it felt almost normal. But the relief was short-lived. My joints throbbed, my breathing felt labored, and a quiet urgency settled in my chest. This was no longer fatigue. This was my body demanding attention.

That evening, I decided to seek guidance rather than push through one more night. I contacted Teladoc, carefully describing the progression of my symptoms. As the doctor listened, her tone shifted—calm, steady, but unmistakably urgent. "You need to go to the ER tonight or first thing in the morning," She said. "These are signs of congestive heart failure."

The words lingered in the air. In that stillness, another familiar scripture surfaced, steadying my breath: "Do you not know that your body is the temple of the Holy Spirit who is in you?" (1 Corinthians 6:19, NKJV). I felt the Holy Spirit confirm them deep within me, encouraging my trust in God's guidance during uncertainty. I knew with sobering clarity that if I lay down that night, I might not wake up in the morning—and that knowing is what compelled me to go to the emergency room.

When we arrived at the emergency room, the waiting area was empty—no lines, no delays. Within minutes, I was rushed through a series of tests. The results came one after another, each more sobering than the last:

- ➢ Heart attack
- ➢ Blood clots in my heart and lungs
- ➢ An enlarged heart
- ➢ An inflamed liver
- ➢ Blood sugar over 300
- ➢ An ejection fraction under 15 percent—critical heart failure, where normal function is above 50 percent

The results were a devastating contradiction to the picture I had of myself. I wasn't overweight. I avoided processed foods. I believed I was healthy. But I was overworked, undernourished, and deeply depleted from years of carrying spiritual and emotional weight.

I was transferred by ambulance to another hospital, where an angiogram confirmed three major blocked arteries. Days later, I was discharged with a regimen of medications—many with severe side effects—and a wearable defibrillator meant to shock my heart if it stopped beating. Yet before I left that hospital, Heaven intervened.

I called my pastor and asked for prayer. In the middle of our conversation, words rose out of me without effort or rehearsal: "My name shall be called Catherine Newheart."

The room shifted. I felt Heaven meet me there. I knew God was giving me a new name, a new identity, and a new assignment. This moment of divine intervention was a powerful reminder that I was being reborn, inspiring faith and hope in my audience.

"You shall be called by a new name, which the mouth of the Lord will name." —Isaiah 62:2 (NKJV)

When Medicine Hurts More Than It Heals

Returning home did not bring immediate relief. The medications caused dizziness, nausea, night sweats, and deep emotional lows. In my desperation, I cried out to God. One Sunday morning, I sensed Him highlight a specific medication. When I researched it, I was stunned to see every symptom I was experiencing listed as a side effect. I knew it was time to seek a new physician.

Appointments were difficult to secure, but I persisted. I advocated for myself while anchoring my faith in Scripture—not to deny the reality of my condition, but to partner with God's healing power alongside medical treatment. The pain didn't vanish overnight, and the diagnosis remained, but my faith took deeper root, reminding me that divine healing can work through both faith and medicine.

When Food Becomes Healing

My healing journey required change on every level. I discovered my body could no longer tolerate sugar, bread, or rice, revealing sensitivities I had never faced before. Releasing familiar comfort foods was challenging, but the process forced me to nourish my body with intention.

Within ninety days of changing how I ate—eliminating nightshades, reducing processed carbohydrates, and focusing on clean foods—I noticed measurable improvement. Inflammation decreased. My digestion settled. My body, long ignored, finally responded.

I studied the work of Dr. Steven Gundry and Dr. Don Colbert, whose teachings challenged conventional approaches to health. When Dr. Gundry said, "What you eat either heals you or kills you," it echoed what the Spirit had already revealed: healing required alignment, not shortcuts.

This Book Is Your Sign

What if this book is the sign you've been asking for? What if these pages mark your own divine interruption—your moment of? **Newheart.**

I don't offer polished theology or sugar-coated stories. I offer lived encounters with God's power—hospital rooms interrupted by Heaven, faith forged under pressure, and a journey from fear to restoration. This book is a testimony of divine healing and supernatural intervention.

You are about to witness a journey that includes hospital beds, tear-soaked pillows, faith-stretching prayers, and divine dreams filled with keys, oil, mantles, and courtroom decrees. You'll learn how faith doesn't ignore pain—it overcomes it. You'll see how I transitioned from hopelessness to healing; not because I had the best doctors, but because I had a God who was not finished writing my story. And by the end of these pages, you won't just believe in miracles. You'll expect them.

God didn't just give me a new heart. He gave me a new name, a new mission, and a new mantle. And now, it's time for you to discover what He's writing over your life.

The journey to healing doesn't begin in the hospital. It begins with awareness. And awareness leads to advocacy. It's the moment you realize you're not helpless—you're powerful because the Spirit of God lives in you. Healing isn't always instant. Sometimes it's a long obedience in the same direction. But with every step, every prayer, every whispered declaration, you are rising. And Heaven is still writing your story.

Why I Wrote This Book

This book isn't just about me. It's about you.

It's for the woman facing chronic illness and praying for one more day. It's for the man who hides his symptoms out of fear. It's for the youth silently suffering in their bodies while crying out for hope. It's for the caregiver on the edge of burnout.

This is your divine interruption. Your invitation to believe again.

I didn't have unlimited resources or access to elite medical care. But I had the Word of God, the name of Jesus, a mustard seed of faith—and a new identity straight from Heaven.

🔍 Reflection Prompts

Have you been ignoring symptoms God is urging you to pay attention to?

Are you over-functioning for others while neglecting your own health?

What divine identity is God speaking over you right now?

What would it look like to stop surviving and start advocating for your healing?

📖 Healing Scriptures

Psalm 73:26 (NIV)

"My flesh and my heart may fail, but God is the strength of my heart and my portion forever."

Jeremiah 30:17 (NIV)

"'But I will restore you to health and heal your wounds,' declares the Lord."

Exodus 15:26b (NLT)

"For I am the Lord who heals you."

Isaiah 43:1 (NIV)

"Do not fear, for I have redeemed you; I have summoned you by name; you are mine."

🙏 Prayer Declaration

Heavenly Father,

You see what no doctor can detect and hear what I cannot articulate.

> Thank you for divine interruptions that redirect and realign.
> Thank you for the moment you renamed me.
> I declare I will live and not die.
> My body will respond to the rhythm of resurrection.
> I refuse to live in fear.
> I embrace your healing and step into my new identity.
> I am not who I used to be.
> I am Catherine Newheart.
> In Jesus' name, Amen.

⚡ Unshakable Charge

Your diagnosis is not your destiny.

Your scars are not signs of defeat—they're signs you survived.

The Spirit of God still breathes life into dry bones.

Declare your healing. Declare your new name.

Stand tall. Heaven is not finished with you.

You are seen.

You are called.

You are **UNSHAKABLE.**

CHAPTER 2

WHEN HEAVEN SENT A PROPHECY

When Medical Devices Become Altars of Faith

There are seasons when God uses the very thing meant to keep you alive to teach you how to truly live. For me, it came in the form of a defibrillator vest—bulky, uncomfortable, and life-saving. Worn day and night after I was released from the hospital, it was designed to detect sudden cardiac arrest and deliver a shock to restart my heart if needed. Every beep was a warning. Every vibration, a reminder: You are still on the edge.

But what man designed to preserve my body, God used to awaken my spirit.

Each night, I lay awake, not just wrapped in that device, but in the divine presence. The weight on my chest was not just a reminder of danger, but of destiny. With every pulse of fear, I whispered scriptures and declarations. That vest was not just a medical device—it became my altar of faith.

15

Here's what terrifies me when I look back: I had been walking around with a heart attack and didn't even know it.

It wasn't until that fateful night of October 15th, 2022—when the Teladoc physician urged me to go to the ER immediately—that doctors discovered the truth. The tests revealed what I had been unknowingly carrying: a silent heart attack, inflamed organs, blood clots, and a dangerously low ejection fraction.

I had chalked up my symptoms to exhaustion. Stress. Maybe the flu. But my body had been screaming warnings I didn't recognize.

And here's the part every woman reading this needs to understand: Heart attacks look different in women.

While men typically experience crushing chest pain and pain radiating down the left arm, women often have what doctors call "atypical" symptoms—symptoms so subtle or confusing that they're dismissed as indigestion, anxiety, or just "being tired."

For me, it was:

Shortness of breath (even without exertion)

Overwhelming fatigue that rest couldn't fix

Nausea and loss of appetite

Swelling in my ankles

Chest tightness that felt more like pressure than pain

I didn't clutch my chest and collapse like you see in the movies. I kept going. I kept serving. I kept pushing through—until my body finally forced me to stop.

Medical studies show that nearly 1 in 3 heart attack patients experience no chest pain at all—and this is far more common in women. These are called "silent heart attacks," and they're just as deadly. By the time many women seek help, the damage is already extensive.

I was one of those women.

And if the Holy Spirit hadn't nudged me to make that call on October 15th, I might not be here to write this.

Christmas in Crisis

In the glow of Christmas lights in December 2022, while others gathered in celebration, I was clinging to life. My body was frail. My appetite was gone. Fatigue sat on my shoulders like a weighted blanket. I'd walk through the house wrapped in both my vest and a prayer shawl, praying, "Lord, let this heart beat with purpose again."

My dining table had become a pharmacy—orange bottles lined up in rows like soldiers. Over a dozen medications, each with side effects worse than the last. One promised to steady my heart but caused nausea so intense I couldn't eat. Another affected my mood, making it difficult to pray, focus, or even believe. A third one caused chest tightness that mimicked the heart attack symptoms all over again.

One Sunday, on my way to church, a sudden chest pain forced me to pull over. A quick check of the medication's side effects revealed I was having an allergic reaction. I whispered a prayer of thanks to God for this understanding. It was clear something had to change, but now I had a direction to move in.

By late December, my family and I were growing increasingly alarmed by my deteriorating state. Yet the Christmas season—normally filled with joy—presented an unusual hurdle. Doctors' offices were closed or short-staffed, and it felt nearly impossible to get a timely appointment. Still, I believed that healing prayers could go hand in hand with proper medical care. My spiritual sister urged, "We need a second opinion." She was right. It was time to fight for my life in a new way—through prayer and persistence.

God's Unlikely Answer

So, we scoured referrals and hospital websites, searching for any cardiologist who would see a new patient on short notice. I prayed over each name that surfaced, asking God to lead me. Finally, one name stood out—Dr. Araj, a highly recommended heart specialist who, miraculously, had an opening on December 28th, squeezed in during that quiet week between Christmas and New Year's.

When I saw his name and background, I paused. Dr. Araj wasn't Christian. He practiced a different faith entirely. For a moment, I wondered if this was the right fit. But the Holy Spirit whispered something profound to my heart:

"I can use anyone. I'm not limited by religion, background, or belief system. I place the right people in your path, and I work through willing hands—no matter whose hands they are."

That revelation was freeing. God was reminding me that He is sovereign over all creation, and He uses whomever He chooses to fulfill His purposes. I needed to be open to how He was orchestrating my healing, even if it looked different than I expected.

With renewed faith, I took the appointment. It felt like a door divinely cracked open.

The Appointment That Changed Everything

On December 28th, 2022, we walked into Dr. Araj's office believing that God had orchestrated this meeting. The winter sun was bright that day, but my body was weak—Cora, my supervisor who had become like a sister to me, practically had to steady me as we checked in. The waiting room was nearly empty; most people were still on holiday, but for me, this was no vacation. A nurse greeted us kindly, and despite the seasonal understaffing, I sensed an unusual peace in that office. It was as if God had cleared a path for me once again.

When Dr. Araj entered the exam room, I was immediately struck by his gentle demeanor. He introduced himself with a warm smile. He didn't rush or keep his eyes glued to a screen as so many others had. Instead, he pulled out a plain notepad and pen. It was old-fashioned, but it felt reassuring—here was a man ready to truly listen. He looked up and said, "Tell me everything from the beginning." And so, I did.

As I spoke, haltingly at times, he listened intently. I told him everything—the silent heart attack I didn't know I'd had, the heart failure diagnosis, the vest I slept in, the mountain of medications, and even the allergic reaction I'd discovered on my own. My voice trembled as I confessed how despair had crept in during what was meant to be a joyful season. He nodded kindly, his eyes never leaving mine.

Every so often, he jotted down a note, but not once did I feel dismissed or unheard. In his face, I saw compassion; in his posture, I sensed respect. For the first time in a long time, I felt seen. It was as though he wasn't just examining a patient; he was truly seeing a person.

Cora came armed with questions—the same supervisor-turned-sister-friend who had been watching over me—and my daughter quietly recorded the session on her phone. Dr. Araj welcomed our thorough approach. He answered everything with patience and never rushed us. It felt as if God Himself had provided a wise counselor for us. The Holy Spirit's presence was palpable, guiding the conversation.

In that moment, I understood: God doesn't need us to stay in our religious boxes. He needs us to stay open to His direction. Dr. Araj may not have shared my faith, but he was undeniably an instrument of divine mercy in my life. His skill, his compassion, and his willingness to truly listen were all gifts from a God who sees beyond our limitations.

The Medication Breakthrough

After a careful physical exam and a review of my hospital records, Dr. Araj turned to the elephant in the room: my towering stack of medications. The nurse had faxed over my prescription list ahead of time, and it ran nearly two pages long. He scanned the list, then uncapped his pen and boldly struck out more than half of them. "You don't need all of these," he said, shaking his head. "They're too strong for your system."

I exhaled the breath I'd been holding. In that instant, Dr. Araj confirmed what my gut already knew: I wasn't failing or crazy—I was over-medicated.

He then carefully reviewed the remaining prescriptions with me. One drug, though standard for many patients, was doing more harm than good in my case, so we would drop it. Another would be reduced to a milder dose to avoid overwhelming my system. I was astonished—no doctor had ever walked me through my treatment like this before. He wasn't just treating my heart; he was empowering my mind.

In that sterile exam room, I received an education in my own health, and it felt liberating. "My people are destroyed for lack of knowledge" (Hosea 4:6) is a warning from Scripture. But knowledge, paired with discernment, becomes a weapon against despair.

Next, he pointed to the one drug that had haunted me for weeks—the medication likely responsible for my allergic reaction. "And this one," he said, drawing a thick line through it, "we're discontinuing immediately." I nearly cried with relief.

That drug had been a shackle on my life. With one stroke of his pen, that shackle was broken. "Therefore, if the Son makes you free, you shall be free indeed" (John 8:36). God used this moment to break more than one chain.

He assured me there were better, gentler alternatives that wouldn't require constant monitoring. By the end, he had whittled my regimen down to a few essential medicines. He gave me a reassuring smile. "I believe this will be much more tolerable for you," he said.

In an hour, Dr. Araj had unraveled weeks of confusion and fear. He handed me a sensible plan and most importantly, a ray of hope that I might feel like myself again soon.

Divine Compassion in Action

As I prepared to leave, the nurse noticed my concern about one of the new (and very expensive) prescriptions. She slipped out for a moment and returned with a manufacturer's coupon that would drastically reduce the cost. That simple act of compassion nearly brought tears to my eyes. It felt like God's love in action, as if He were saying, I've got this covered, too.

Cora and my daughter helped me out of the clinic after the visit, their faces alight with more optimism than I'd seen in months. As we drove away, the car was filled with a quiet, joyful awe. We knew we had witnessed something sacred. I felt a new spark of life in my chest.

The defibrillator vest strapped to me—once only a reminder of death averted—now felt like a promise of life to come. The very mechanism meant to save my life had become something sacred. Every time I touched the bulky vest, I remembered the goodness of God in leading me to that doctor. What had been a symbol of crisis was now an emblem of hope.

Faith Without Borders

In a sense, that defibrillator became my altar of faith: I decided that every day I wore it, I would thank God for the gift of another day and dedicate each heartbeat to Him. "Teach us to number our days, that we may gain a heart of wisdom" (Psalm 90:12). I was learning what it meant to truly live, choosing faith over fear.

I also realized that being my own advocate was crucial. Yes, we trust doctors, but we must also listen to the nudges of the Holy Spirit within us. I'm alive today because I heeded those divine whispers—seeking a second opinion, researching side effects, not settling for suffering, and remaining open to how God might answer my prayers, even if it came through unexpected hands.

I learned that faith isn't passive—sometimes faith means speaking up, asking questions, knocking on one more door when others have closed, and trusting that God is bigger than our religious boundaries. "Ask and it will be given to you; seek and you will find; knock and the door will be opened to you" (Matthew 7:7).

On the drive home, I realized this chapter of my life wasn't about a diagnosis at all—it was about destiny. I had learned to trust God's gentle whispers and believe His Word over the bleak reports. What the enemy had meant for harm, God was turning for good.

My story was being rewritten by the Author of Life. I was no longer just a heart patient; I now had a mission to live and declare the works of the Lord. "You are my hiding place and my shield; I hope in Your word" (Psalm 119:114).

The word that echoed in my spirit was Unshakable. That's what God was building in me—an unshakable faith that no trial could destroy. The vest on my body, the prescriptions in my hand, even the name "Newheart" I now carried—each was a thread in the tapestry of grace, living evidence that Heaven still rewrites stories.

Truly, God was giving me a new heart in more ways than one: "I will give you a new heart and put a new spirit in you," He promised (Ezekiel 36:26). I was living proof that no diagnosis could ever define me more than God's promise could.

A Word To Women Readers

If you're reading this and experiencing:

Unexplained fatigue that rest doesn't fix

Shortness of breath during normal activities

Nausea or loss of appetite

Jaw, neck, or back pain

Chest pressure (not necessarily pain)

Swelling in ankles or legs

Please don't dismiss it. Don't wait. Don't assume it's "just stress."

Heart disease is the #1 killer of women, and we are far more likely than men to experience subtle symptoms that get brushed off—by ourselves and sometimes even by medical professionals.

Trust your body. Advocate for yourself. Ask for tests. Get a second opinion.

Your life is worth fighting for.

🔍 Reflection Prompts

Where have you been relying solely on doctors or human knowledge without seeking divine wisdom?

What fears have been whispering that your condition is final?

Can you recall a moment when God sent someone unexpectedly to strengthen your faith—perhaps someone who didn't fit your expectations?

In what ways is God asking you to step out in faith before you see the miracle?

Are you open to receiving God's help through unexpected sources?

🕊 Healing Scriptures

Psalm 30:2 (NKJV) "O Lord my God, I cried to You for help, and You healed me."

Jeremiah 30:17 (NKJV) "'For I will restore health to you and heal you of your wounds,' says the Lord."

Jeremiah 33:6 (NIV) "But I will bring health and healing to it; I will heal my people and let them enjoy abundant peace and security."

Psalm 107:20 (NKJV) "He sent His word and healed them, and delivered them from their destructions."

1 Peter 2:24 (NKJV) "By His wounds you have been healed."

🙏 Prayer Declaration

Father in Heaven,

I thank you that you are the Great Physician, the one who sees every diagnosis and every cell in my body. I release every fear and place my full trust in You. I renounce the voice of doubt and stand on the unshakable truth of Your Word. You are Jehovah Rapha—my Healer, my Restorer, my Source.

Even when doctors say no, you still say yes. I receive divine wisdom, strength, and peace. Send the right voices into my life, Lord—even unexpected ones. Align me with helpers, healers, and holy strategies, no matter where they come from. I declare that healing is mine—not by might or power, but by Your Spirit.

In Jesus' mighty name, Amen.

⚡ Unshakable Charge

You are not at the mercy of man's report. The final word belongs to God. He is rewriting your story, redirecting your path, and rebuilding your strength. Don't settle for survival—press in for total healing.

God is not limited by borders, backgrounds, or beliefs. He can use anyone to deliver your breakthrough. Stay open. Stay expectant. Stay obedient.

This is not your end. This is your turning point.

You are **UNSHAKABLE.**

CHAPTER 3

THE ARSENALS OF HEAVEN

When Sickness Attacked, My Spirit Fought Back

Spiritual warfare, in its truest form, isn't always loud and dramatic. It's a silent struggle, waged in the stillness— whispered in the dark when pain jolts you awake at 3 a.m. and fear tries to convince you that dawn may never come. Understanding how this applies to health battles helps believers see their struggles as part of spiritual warfare, encouraging them to use faith as a weapon.

My body was shutting down. Doctors had painted a grim picture: heart failure, blood clots, a dangerously low ejection fraction. But in the chaos of their words, a calm rose inside of me— not because of denial, but because I knew this wasn't the end. Though my body was weak, my spirit was fierce. I knew I had to fight. And my weapons weren't natural—they were spiritual.

"For the weapons of our warfare are not carnal, but mighty through God to the pulling down of strongholds." —2 Corinthians 10:4

When I returned home after one of my many hospital stays, my body was frail and shaking. I could barely walk from the bed to the bathroom. My heartbeat was erratic. Swallowing even water felt like drinking shards of glass. I chose to fight, and I was losing weight rapidly. The life I once led—speaking, leading, serving—felt like a distant dream. Yet, in that quiet space, I chose to fight, igniting a sense of empowerment in others facing their own battles.

Though my strength was depleted, I declared aloud, "This is not where my story ends. God still writes my chapters." To do this effectively, I learned to activate my spiritual weapons-speaking scriptures, worship, and prayer—deliberately during my battles, inspiring others to do the same in their struggles.

Weapon 1: The Word of God—My Sword and Shield

Every corner of my home became a sanctuary of faith. Scriptures adorned mirrors, doorframes, cabinets, and even lampshades. I needed the Word to envelop me, to saturate my surroundings with truth and hope.

Isaiah 53:5 was taped to my bedpost: "By His stripes I am healed."

Psalm 107:20 sat on my kitchen counter: "He sent His Word and healed them."

Psalm 118:17 was on my front door: "I shall not die, but live, and declare the works of the Lord."

Even when I couldn't pray aloud, the Word spoke on my behalf. It preached to my weary bones. It fought battles my body couldn't. The Bible says His Word is living, active, and sharper than any two-edged sword (Hebrews 4:12). That sword became my lifeline.

Weapon 2: Praise—The Sound That Shattered Silence

Praise wasn't a luxury—it was my lifeline. I filled my space with worship music, Healing Scriptures, and teachings by spiritual leaders. Even when my voice faltered, my spirit sang.

I'd whisper: "I will bless the Lord at all times; His praise shall continually be in my mouth" (Psalm 34:1). Praise wasn't dependent on how I felt; it was a weapon and a battle cry.

Weapon 3: Prayer—My Constant Cry

My prayers were not scripted; they were raw, holy groans. I wept, I pleaded, I shouted, I whispered. And I prayed without ceasing.

I called every prayer line I could find—Andrew Womack Ministries, Terradez Ministries, Fire Altar NSPPD. Strangers across time zones became my intercessors. Their prayers became a chorus of faith pushing back the darkness.

"Men ought always to pray, and not faint." —Luke 18:1

I didn't pray because I was strong. I prayed because I had no strength left. And that made the prayers more powerful.

Weapon 4: Fasting—Starving the Flesh, Feeding the Spirit

Even though I was already frail, the Lord led me to fast. Not recklessly, but sacrificially. Some days it was food. On other days, it was social media, conversations, or entertainment. My mentor fasted with me. Together, we warred in the spirit.

Each fast sharpened my ears to heaven. I could sense God's presence like never before. He gave me instructions—what to eat, what to avoid, what to declare, and how to rest.

Weapon 5: Anointing Oil—A Tangible Act of Faith

I anointed everything.

My forehead—"I have the mind of Christ."

My chest—"God is giving me a new heart."

My bed—"This is not a grave but a healing place."

My oxygen machine and the defibrillator vest—"This is temporary. Healing is permanent."

"Is anyone among you sick? Let them call the elders… and pray over them, anointing them with oil in the name of the Lord." — James 5:14

Though no elders were physically present, the Holy Spirit was. And that oil? It wasn't superstition. It was faith in action, a tangible reminder that spiritual weapons like anointing oil are powerful tools God has given us to fight battles, even when circumstances seem impossible.

Weapon 6: Testimony—Speaking Faith in Real Time

I didn't wait until I was completely healed to testify. I shared in real time. In Uber rides, In hospital waiting rooms., with pharmacy clerks and grocery store employees.

Every "God is healing me" was a prophetic blow to the enemy's lies. Revelation 12:11 says, "They overcame by the blood of the Lamb and the word of their testimony." I was living proof.

Weapon 7: Unity—A Global Army of Faith

What I lacked in strength, others supplied. My daughter stood in the gap. WHOZ leaders surrounded me with intercession. Women laid hands on me, washed my feet, and declared the Word over me.

Their prayers formed a spiritual shield wall. Psalm 133:1 says, "How good and pleasant it is when God's people live together in unity." I felt that unity. I lived that unity. It carried me when I couldn't carry myself.

Weapon 8: The Blood of Jesus—The Ultimate Covering

The last weapon—the Blood of Jesus—was the most powerful of all. I began to plead the Blood over my body, my home, my daughter, and every organ in my system.

"And they overcame him by the blood of the Lamb..." — Revelation 12:11

There is no force more powerful than the Blood. It not only covers sin—it heals sickness, silences accusation, and destroys demonic assignments.

I anointed my bed, declaring, "By His Blood, I sleep in peace."

I touched the doorposts of my home, saying, "No plague shall enter here. I am covered." (Exodus 12:13)

The Blood became my banner. My medicine. My defense. My confidence.

🔍 Reflection Prompts

Are you fighting your battles with spiritual weapons or worldly ones?

Have you filled your atmosphere with the Word or with worry?

Are you surrounded by intercessors or suffering in silence?

🕊 Healing Scriptures

Isaiah 54:17 (NKJV)"No weapon formed against you shall prosper."

Ephesians 6:10 (NKJV)"Be strong in the Lord and in the power of His might."

Psalm 50:15 (NKJV)"Call upon Me in the day of trouble; I will deliver you."

🙏 Prayer Declaration

Heavenly Father,

Thank you for reminding me that I am not powerless in this battle. You have equipped me with divine weapons—truth, faith, the Word, worship, and prayer. I silence every voice of fear and declare that You are my shield and defender. Let praise rise from my lips. Let healing flood my body. I put on the full armor of God. I speak life. I declare breakthrough. I declare victory in Jesus Name

⚡ Unshakable Charge

Spiritual warfare is not for the elite—it's for you. It's for every mother, father, child, and warrior navigating pain and uncertainty.

You are not weaponless. You are not alone. Stand firm. Speak boldly. Worship deeply. Fight spiritually. You are not helpless. God has given you everything you need to stand. Even in the valley, you have the victory. Pick up your sword. Lift your voice. Plead the Blood.

You are armed. You are chosen.

You are **UNSHAKABLE.**

CHAPTER 4

DREAMS FROM THE THRONE ROOM

When Heaven Spoke in Visions

I want to share how divine messages have shaped my faith journey to inspire others to trust God's guidance.

I have always been a dreamer. Not the head-in-the-clouds kind, but the kind who wakes up at 3 a.m. with images still burning behind her eyelids, knowing what she just saw was a direct message from God. Once I dreamed of myself in a new role, doing something I had never done before. When I woke up, I looked at my qualifications and circumstances and talked myself out of it. But I learned a critical lesson: when God shows you something, acting in faith can open new doors, inspiring hope and trust in divine guidance.

The First Key Dream

Years before my heart failed, God used a dream at work to teach me to pay attention. In the dream, I was at the ministry where I had served for more than two decades. Everyone—including the CEO—stood outside the building. The doors were locked. The CEO paced, distressed. "We can't get in," someone said. "The key is lost."

In the dream, I took off running around the building. On the far side, hidden in the grass near a back entrance, I saw it—a single key. I picked it up, ran back, and handed it to the CEO. He turned it in the lock. The doors opened. Everyone went inside.

I journaled the dream and wondered what it meant. Two weeks later, our organization faced a serious financial audit. People were anxious. The CEO looked shaken. I quietly told a leader, "I had a dream that the key was found. We're going to be okay." A few days later, the missing documentation surfaced, and the audit cleared. Once again, the "door" opened.

That experience marked me: when God shows you keys, He is giving you access to His promises and plans. Recognizing divine keys can strengthen your confidence that God is actively providing for your needs and opening spiritual doors.

Courtroom of Heaven (The Verdict)

Fast-forward to one of my darkest nights. I had been home from the hospital for two weeks. The medications were making me sicker than the heart failure. I could not eat. I could not sleep. My strength was almost gone. That night, I collapsed into bed and prayed a prayer I had never prayed before: "God, if You are going to take me, just take me. I cannot do this anymore." It was not suicidal. It was a complete surrender.

I fell asleep. And everything shifted.

In the spirit, I was running toward a majestic courtroom, symbolizing God's authority and His power to judge and bring victory over my circumstances.

At the foot of its stone steps, the weakness from my real body tried to bleed into the dream. My legs felt heavy. My chest tightened. But I knew I had to get inside. I gathered every ounce of faith and began to climb. One step. Two. Three. Each felt like a mountain, but I kept going until I reached the top.

The doors opened. I walked in.

The courtroom took my breath away. The walls rose like crystal and light woven together. The air pulsed with holiness.

The moment I stepped inside, my body reacted before my mind could catch up. I dropped to the floor and began rolling from one end of the courtroom to the other—not crawling, not walking, but rolling in worship that bypassed language. My spirit groaned prayers my mouth could not form. Tears streamed down my face. I was undone.

Then I heard it—a voice, not audible but unmistakable. "Pick her up."

Hands—strong, gentle, unseen—lifted me. I stood facing the front. The Judge sat at the bench. I could not see His face; the light was too bright, too pure. But I knew it was Jesus—no longer only the gentle Shepherd, but the righteous Judge, clothed in authority and radiating power.

To my surprise, I approached the bench. Not timid. Not apologetic. Bold. Desperate.

"I have adversaries," I said, my voice steady. "Sickness. Death. Fear. The enemy himself. They are coming for my life. They are trying to destroy me. But I am Your child, and I ask You—Judge of Heaven and earth—to rule on my behalf."

The courtroom fell silent. Then He lifted the gavel.

BANG. The sound reverberated through the room—and through my chest, into the natural realm where my LifeVest still hummed.

BANG. A second strike, deeper.

BANG. A third.

The verdict was not spoken in sentences, but my spirit knew: Your adversaries are judged. The case is closed. You will live.

I woke up gasping. The LifeVest was still strapped to me. The clock read 2:33 a.m. Princess slept in the next room. Nothing in the natural looked different. But everything in the unseen had shifted. Heaven had ruled.

The Wallet and the Keys (The Practical Instruction)

About a week later, another dream came—this one preceded by a very specific prayer. I had just returned from yet another ER visit. My heart raced with severe palpitations. I could not keep food down. Doctors had ordered another MRI to investigate sharp, needle-like pain in my stomach. The scans showed nothing. I went home with stronger pain medicine, aching muscles, and no answers.

I tried to transfer my care to a Christian homeopathic doctor I had found, but his clinic was far away. In my condition, driving that distance felt impossible. I was tired—tired of tests, tired of not knowing, tired of being sick.

That night I prayed, "Jesus, I need You to guide me. Show me what to do. Give me a key." Then I went to bed.

In the dream, I was standing in my home. I opened my wallet, and inside were a set of keys. Beside them was a clear picture of over-the-counter heart supplements: CoQ10 and omega-3.

When I woke up, the images were still vivid. I did not dismiss them as random. I recognized the Holy Spirit's answer to the prayer I had prayed the night before. My healing would be near, affordable, and attainable. This was a key I could actually use.

That very day I began taking CoQ10 and omega-3. To this day, I still do. The dream did not replace my doctors, but it gave me a practical step and a reminder: God knew exactly where I was, what I could afford, and what my body needed. He put the "keys" where I would see them—in my wallet.

That revelation changed everything. I was not waiting on Heaven; Heaven was waiting on me to walk through the door. I did not need to earn access—I already held the keys. From then on, my prayers shifted from begging to bold declarations.

Not every dream was comforting. One night I stood at the edge of a wide river. The water was dark and fast. On the far side was land—green, lush, vibrant—everything I had been fighting for. Between me and that shore was a massive python, coiled in the water, its black scales glistening, its eyes locked on me.

It did not strike; it simply blocked the crossing. Its presence spoke: You'll never make it. You're too weak. You might survive, but you'll never truly thrive.

Then another voice rose within my spirit—the Holy Spirit: "Strike its head."

Though no weapon was visible, a sword suddenly appeared in my hand, and I struck the serpent with all my might, hitting its head. The serpent recoiled, thrashed, and then disintegrated. The waters calmed, and I crossed to the other side.

When I woke up, Psalm 91 was burning in my heart: "You shall tread upon the lion and the cobra…"

The python was more than a snake; it was intimidation and spiritual opposition trying to convince me I would always live on the edge of death. God was showing me that what I conquer in the spirit will manifest in the natural. I would have to fight for my healing—but victory was already mine.

"Take Pictures. They Won't Believe It."

Near dawn on another morning, I heard the Holy Spirit speak as clearly as if someone were standing beside my bed: "Take pictures of yourself. They won't believe it."

I looked in the mirror and almost argued. My body was emaciated and discolored. My feet were swollen. I looked like a shadow of the woman I used to be. But the instruction was clear, so I obeyed.

I took pictures of my face, my feet, the rows of pill bottles, the LifeVest strapped to my chest. I dated each one and saved them in a folder on my phone labeled "Before."

I was not documenting defeat. I was collecting evidence.

Today, those photos speak louder than any description. God did not just stabilize me; He transformed me. The "before" makes the "after" undeniable.

Stewarding the Dreams

I did not treat any of these divine encounters casually. I wrote them down. Some led me to fast. Some led to divine connections—people who would play crucial roles in my healing journey. Others exposed strongholds that needed to be broken. None of those encounters were coincidence; they were part of God's strategy for my healing and growth.

Dreams require discernment. Some are for intercession, some for obedience, and some for testimony.

When God speaks in the night, wise ones listen with open hearts and take action in the daylight.

There Is a Realm Beyond This One

These dreams reminded me that the natural realm is not all there is. We live in two realms—the seen and the unseen. Angels were warring on my behalf. Courts in Heaven were issuing rulings. Weapons were being placed in my hands. Doors were opening with keys from the Spirit.

Victory begins in the spirit. When Heaven speaks, we must respond. The healing, guidance, and deliverance you are praying for may already be in your spirit. Ask God to awaken your spiritual senses, and trust Him to reveal the mysteries that belong to you.

"The secret things belong to the Lord our God, but those things which are revealed belong to us and to our children forever..." —Deuteronomy 29:29 (NKJV)

🔍 Reflections Prompts

Are you paying attention to your dreams?

Are you recording them?

Are you acting on them?

The healing, guidance, and deliverance you're praying for may already be in your spirit. Ask God to activate your spiritual senses.

Have you asked the Holy Spirit to guide you in interpreting your dreams?

Is there a recent dream that might contain hidden guidance for your healing or next step?

🕊 Healing Scriptures

"Yea, though I walk through the valley of the shadow of death, I will fear no evil; for You are with me; Your rod and Your staff, they comfort me." — Psalm 23:4

"He sent His word and healed them, and delivered them from their destructions." — Psalm 107:20

"In the last days… your sons and daughters will prophesy, your young men will see visions, your old men will dream dreams." — Acts 2:17

"Call to Me and I will answer you and show you great and unsearchable things you do not know." — Jeremiah 33:3

🙏 Prayer Declaration

Father,

Thank you for speaking to your children through dreams, visions, and the whispers of your Spirit. Open my ears to hear You in the night and my eyes to see the unseen. I ask for divine discernment, clarity, and obedience. Let every dream I receive be sealed in Your Spirit and aligned with Your Word.

I will not dismiss divine instruction. I will steward your mysteries well.

Let every ruling from the Heavenly courtroom be manifested in my body, mind, and life.

I declare that my healing is decreed, my destiny is unlocked, and my steps are ordered.

In Jesus' powerful name, Amen.

⚡ Unshakable Charge

You are not alone in the dark.

Heaven is speaking.

Dreams are downloads. Visions are instructions.

Pay attention. Write them down. Act in faith.

You are not waiting for favor—you already have it.

You are **UNSHAKABLE.**

CHAPTER 5

THE VALLEY OF FRAILTY

When Weakness Becomes the Stage for God's Strength

There's a difference between being sick and being frail.

Frailty is a different kind of battle—the slow erosion of strength, independence, and identity. In the Valley of Frailty, I was no longer the helper; I became the one in need. Yet even in that vulnerable place, God's voice broke through louder than the silence of despair. His whispers of comfort reminded me He never left me. It is in these moments of vulnerability that our faith finds hope, knowing God's strength is greater than our weakness.

When Daily Tasks Became Mountains

I remember the first time I couldn't walk from my bedroom to the kitchen without stopping to catch my breath. Just a few steps felt like a marathon. Showers drained me. Carrying groceries was impossible. I struggled even to open a jar. It was terrifying.

I had spent decades serving others. As a caregiver, a leader, and a mother, my life was poured out. But now? Now I needed help brushing my hair.

My daughter, while managing college and her job, quietly took on more. She cooked. She cleaned. She helped me dress. She never once complained. Her strength in silence inspired me to fight harder.

But my body wouldn't cooperate. I had to "budget" my energy. Get dressed, rest. Wash a dish, sit down. Life became a series of calculated surrenders, and each small task became an act of courage.

When Pride and Pain Collide

The most painful battles weren't physical. They were emotional.

Pride whispered that I should hide. That people would pity me. That I had lost my value.

I broke down the first time I used a motorized cart at the grocery store. I sobbed when someone offered to carry my bags. I avoided mirrors because I didn't recognize the woman staring back at me.

Then a stranger approached and softly said, "God bless you." My first instinct was to disappear. But God wouldn't let me.

He spoke to me so gently, "You are not what you do. You are who I say you are."

It shattered me in the best way.

God was breaking off my pride so I could learn humility. So, others could experience compassion. So, I could finally rest and receive. Letting others serve me didn't make me weak. It gave them the honor of standing beside a miracle in motion.

When Food Hurts More Than It Helps

My body was wasting away. Nothing I ate sat well. Carbs caused bloating. Sugar spiked my glucose. Bread, rice, pasta—staples in my upbringing—now made me violently ill.

My digestive system was compromised. My stomach was paralyzed. I was losing weight fast. Even my doctor was alarmed.

Then I remembered a testimony I heard years ago: Jordan Rubin's healing story. I sought out his organic, preservative-free protein powder. It was a start. Then a nutritionist recommended Kate Farms: a plant-based liquid nutrition. It was expensive, but it worked. Within weeks, my blood sugar levels stabilized without the need for insulin. My labs improved. Even my skeptical endocrinologist ran my bloodwork twice—he couldn't believe it.

Divine Wisdom Meets Functional Medicine

God began sending more resources.

I discovered teachings by Dr. Don Colbert and Dr. Steven Gundry. I learned about inflammation, gut health, and the hidden dangers of lectins and nightshades. I eliminated tomatoes, eggplants, gluten, and potatoes.

There were no fireworks. No sudden energy spike. But inside? Something was shifting.

I was walking in obedience, and my body responded. Healing was unfolding in layers. Slowly. Quietly. Faithfully.

Becoming My Own Advocate

I realized another key: I had to advocate for my own healing.

I began researching every prescription. I refused to blindly accept treatments. I prayed, studied, and asked questions. I called prayer lines: Andrew Womack Ministries, Creflo Dollar, Terradez Ministries. They called me back. They prayed. And I held on.

Every night, I played Healing Scriptures in my room. Every morning, I laid hands on my body and declared life.

I remembered Romans 12:2: "Be transformed by the renewing of your mind." Healing was more than physical; it encompassed spiritual, emotional, and mental aspects. And healing is the children's bread (Matthew 15:26).

The Unexpected Gifts in the Valley

This valley stripped me down. But it also built me up.

I gained compassion for those with invisible illnesses. I gained gratitude for the strength to stand, to cook, to breathe. I gained perspective—that my worth wasn't in what I could do, but in who I was in Christ.

Psalm 138:8 became my anchor: "The Lord will perfect that which concerns me."

I found myself clinging to 2 Corinthians 12:9: "My grace is sufficient for you, for My strength is made perfect in weakness."

In the moments I couldn't even lift a fork or button my shirt, I discovered God's strength was not just sufficient—it was shining through.

I had reached the end of me.

And found the beginning of Him.

Teaching Moment: The Healing Journey Is Not Linear

Healing is not a straight line. It is not always instant. It is not always public.

Sometimes it is slow. Sometimes it is private. Sometimes it is painful.

But always—it is holy.

Every meal became obedience. Every breath became worship. Every small improvement was a miracle.

So don't be discouraged. Don't despise your journey.

The valley is not the end; it's the preparation for your comeback.

🔍 Reflections Prompts

What key has God revealed to you lately, through dreams, prayer, or insight?

Is there an area of your life (food, mindset, medication) you need to surrender?

How is God inviting you to be your own advocate?

Are you allowing others to walk beside you?

What "unexpected gifts" has your valley revealed?

🕊 Healing Scriptures

"He sent His word and healed them, and delivered them from their destructions." — Psalm 107:20

"Healing is the children's bread." — Matthew 15:26

"The Lord will perfect that which concerns me." — Psalm 138:8

"My grace is sufficient for you, for My strength is made perfect in weakness." — 2 Corinthians 12:9

"Even though I walk through the valley of the shadow of death, I will fear no evil, for You are with me." — Psalm 23:4

🙏 Prayer Declaration

Father, thank You for walking with me through the Valley of Frailty. When I had no strength, you were my strength. When I couldn't speak, you heard my groans. When I couldn't eat, you became my bread. I declare that I will not fear, because You are with me. I receive the keys you've placed in my hands; wisdom, nutrition, faith, revelation, and rest. Heal me from the inside out, layer by layer. Let the world see your glory through my scars. I will not shrink. I will not hide. I will rise. In Jesus' name, amen.

⚡ Unshakable Charge

Your frailty is not your finale; it's the foundation for a greater strength. God's glory is made perfect not in your might, but in your surrender. Rise daily, even if only in your Spirit. Refuse shame. Embrace rest. Partner with heaven.

Declare healing. Let your valley become your victory.

You are not forgotten.

You are fortified.

You are **UNSHAKABLE.**

CHAPTER 6

VIA DOLOROSA

Walking The Way Of Suffering Into Healing

There are moments in life when suffering becomes more than pain—it becomes sacred. The hospital room had become my personal Gethsemane. The monitors beeped steadily, but my body was anything but stable. Inflammation had ballooned my stomach until I looked several months pregnant, even though I was frail and emaciated everywhere else. My digestive system was shutting down. I couldn't eat. I couldn't swallow pills. Even water refused to stay down.

The weight of weakness sat on my chest like a stone, and then the Holy Spirit whispered: "Via Dolorosa," reminding me of Jesus' path of surrender and divine purpose, which resonated deeply with my suffering.

I knew that phrase. I remembered it from my Catholic roots: The Way of Sorrows, the road Jesus walked to the Cross, symbolizing a spiritual journey of surrender and divine purpose that resonated deeply with my suffering.

Suffering That Sanctifies

In the Western world, we often try to medicate suffering before we interpret it. But recognizing that some suffering is divine can transform our perspective and strengthen our faith.

Isaiah 48:10 (NIV) declares, "I have refined you, though not as silver; I have tested you in the furnace of affliction." The furnace is not fun, but it is necessary. I wasn't being punished. I was being purified.

This experience is a powerful Christian suffering testimony that shows how perseverance in affliction can lead to profound spiritual growth, encouraging others to endure with faith.

The Medical Mystery: When Food Became the Enemy

Despite following a strict, clean, sugar-free, anti-inflammatory diet, I kept declining. My blood sugar had stabilized, but my stomach swelled unnaturally. My body seemed to be at war with itself.

Eventually, I received a diagnosis that explained everything: Helicobacter pylori (H. pylori). It's a bacterial infection that eats away at the stomach's lining, creating ulcers, chronic inflammation, and digestive shutdown. The infection had silently taken root, causing unbearable bloating, nausea, malabsorption, and inflammation. I could barely walk. My spine ached because of rapid muscle loss. My weight was plummeting, but my abdomen looked distended like I was carrying a child of sorrow.

Additionally, further tests revealed esophageal thinning—my swallowing reflex was deteriorating. Doctors began using the term esophageal paralysis, a condition where the muscles that push food from the mouth to the stomach stop working properly. I was told surgery was too risky in my condition. I was slowly wasting away.

A Crisis Before the Catheterization

As if that weren't enough, I was scheduled for a heart catheterization—a diagnostic procedure where doctors insert a thin tube into the heart through blood vessels to evaluate blockages or heart function. How could I undergo a heart procedure if I couldn't even swallow water?

Despite the overwhelming fear, I found emotional strength in my faith. I whispered to God, "If You don't show up, I don't know how I'll make it through this." It was my faith that empowered me to face the unknown with courage, knowing that He was with me every step of the way. This faith, amid fear, is a testament to the transformative power of belief in God's presence.

Heaven Sent Reinforcements (Divine Healing Miracle)

Then, a text from Mary, my ARMI Regional Leader, brought a ray of hope. She had sent out a prayer request to leaders across the nation. One prayer in particular stood out: it reminded me of the woman with the issue of blood, the one who pushed past cultural barriers and physical weakness just to touch the hem of Jesus' garment (Mark 5:25-34).

Mary's words cut deep: "It's your desperation that qualifies you."

That very week, Curry Blake, overseer of John G. Lake Ministries—known for divine healing—unexpectedly appeared at my hospital bed, a powerful reminder of God's miraculous ways and His active involvement in our lives.

Yes, I had called his prayer line months ago. But I never expected him to appear in person. Yet there he was, sent by God. He walked in with quiet authority, carrying the fragrance of Heaven. He laid his hands on me, prayed a bold prayer, anointed me with oil, and looked me square in the eyes.

"You will live and not die. Go through with the procedure."

In that moment, I felt a shift. A surge of peace. A mantle of courage. The Spirit of God used that moment to reroute my fear. This shift in mindset, from fear to peace, is a powerful testament to the transformative power of trusting in God's plan.

The Via Dolorosa Becomes the Via Gloriosa

When you walk through fire and don't smell like smoke, that's God.

As I was prepped for the April 18 heart catheterization, I had no certainty of the outcome. But I had peace. "Via Dolorosa," the Spirit whispered again.

I realized that my journey wasn't a detour; it was a deliberate path. A divine appointment. Jesus walked the Via Dolorosa on His way to redemption. I was walking it as part of mine.

Romans 8:17 reminds us, "If we are to share His glory, we must also share His suffering." But the promise is this: resurrection always follows crucifixion.

The results of the catheterization weren't ideal—my heart showed signs of worsening dysfunction. But I wasn't afraid. Why? Because the storm inside me had been replaced by the peace of God within me.

Medical Insight for Readers

This memoir is also a mirror. So here are the key things I learned:

Condition Explanation & Reader Tip

What is H. pylori?

A common but dangerous bacterial infection that causes ulcers and disrupts digestion. It is often contracted through contaminated food or water and can go undetected for years.

Tip: If you're experiencing unexplained bloating, chronic indigestion, or trouble swallowing, ask your doctor for a breath test for H. pylori.

What is Esophageal Paralysis?

A weakening of the muscles that push food down your throat. It can cause choking, regurgitation, and nutritional deficiencies. Tip: Advocate for yourself. Don't let strange symptoms go unchecked. You are not imagining it.

What is a Heart Catheterization?

A test that checks for blocked arteries, heart damage, and heart function. It's minimally invasive but requires you to be stable.

Tip: If you're scheduled for this test, ask your doctor for preparation instructions. Bring someone with you who can ask questions and take notes.

Sacred Suffering, Glorious Outcome

This chapter of my life redefined what it means to walk with God. I didn't just need a healing. I needed a revelation. God showed me that the Via Dolorosa is not a punishment—it's a pathway to power.

Psalm 34:18 says, "The Lord is close to the brokenhearted and saves those who are crushed in spirit." I was broken, yes—but I was also being carried.

Songs in the Night

During some of my darkest nights in the hospital, God would give me songs—melodies that would rise in my spirit even when I couldn't speak. Psalm 42:8 says, "By day the Lord directs his love, at night his song is with me."

I didn't know this kind of intimacy with God was possible until pain stripped everything away.

These were not polished worship songs. They were raw cries of faith:

🎵 "You are still God in this fire."

🎵 "Even now, you are healing me."

🎵 "This pain is not pointless. It's a path."

I began to write them down, hum them aloud, and let them minister to my soul. In the midnight hour, when no nurse or family member could comfort me, His song wrapped around my heart like a blanket of fire.

🔍 Reflections Prompts

What if your deepest sorrow is also your sacred sanctification?

What if pain is the furnace that shapes your mantle?

What if this "delay" is actually divine preparation?

You may be walking your own Via Dolorosa. Don't resist the process. The Cross wasn't the end for Jesus, and it's not the end for you.

🕊 Healing Scriptures

📖 Isaiah 48:10 – "I have refined you... In the furnace of affliction."

📖 2 Corinthians 4:17 – "These light afflictions... are working for us a far more exceeding weight of glory."

📖 Mark 5:34 – "Daughter, your faith has made you whole."

📖 Psalm 42:8 – "His song is with me in the night."

🙏 Prayer Declaration

Lord, I may be walking through the fire, but I declare You are with me. This path of pain is not a prison—it's a portal. I trust you. Refine me. Purify me. Strengthen me. Let my weakness become the altar where Your strength is made perfect. I declare: I will live and not die. I am not forsaken. I am mantled with glory. In Jesus' name, amen.

⚡ Unshakable Charge

You are not forgotten. You are not cursed. The suffering you're walking through is producing something eternal. This is your Via Dolorosa—but resurrection is coming. Hold fast. Let the fire forge your faith. Let the tears water the soil of your next season. God is working in your weakness.

Don't just endure—press in.

Don't just cry—prophesy.

Don't just survive—declare your healing.

You are **UNSHAKABLE.**

CHAPTER 7

FINAL VERDICT

When Medicine Meets Its Limits

There are moments in life when human expertise reaches its boundaries—when medical knowledge encounters its limitations, and divine intervention becomes the only hope left. That moment came for me in a sterile hospital room, where my surgeon delivered what felt like a final verdict on my life.

"Mrs. Catherine," he began, his voice carrying the weight of clinical professionalism and quiet compassion, "we've reviewed your heart catheterization results. We've considered every surgical option and consulted with our top specialists. I have to be honest with you—we've reached the limit of what we can do medically."

Then came the words that knocked the breath out of me: "Your ejection fraction is still below 25 percent. Given your current condition, you have about a 15% chance of survival." It was Father's Day, June 18, 2023, when I received this devastating news. This moment could have crushed my spirit, but I chose to see it as a challenge to my faith, inspiring hope in my audience that even bleak reports can be met with divine hope.

Fifteen percent. Not fifty. Not even twenty. Fifteen.

It echoed in the room like a sentence being read aloud. My daughter, Princess, squeezed my hand tightly—I could feel her trembling. I understood exactly what that meant: an ejection fraction (EF) is the measure of how effectively the heart pumps blood, and mine was barely hanging on at a critically low level. The odds of survival for an EF this low are bleak.

The doctor continued, gently but plainly. "You are not a good candidate for bypass surgery or even a stent. Your heart is too weak. The risk of surgery is too great. All we can do now is try to keep you stable and comfortable."

The unspoken message was painfully clear: they were managing my dying, not fighting for my living.

Yet deep inside, something else awakened—a holy defiance and a hope that refused to accept the doctor's verdict as the final Word. I looked the doctor in the eye and said, "I serve a God who specializes in impossible cases. That 15% is more than enough for Him to work with."

From Victim to Victor

That night, I made a decision that changed everything. I chose to reject the victim mentality that this diagnosis was trying to impose on me. Instead of asking, 'Why me?' I started declaring, 'Why not me?' This shift in perspective filled me with hope and a renewed sense of purpose, empowering my faith and courage.

I took out my journal and wrote: Today, June 18, 2023, medicine said I have a 15% chance. But I serve the God of 100% victories. Today, doctors said there are no options left. But I know the God of infinite possibilities. Today, the verdict was delivered. But I appeal to a higher court—the Court of Heaven, where Jesus is my advocate and His blood speaks better things than my diagnosis, filling me with confidence in divine power.

Psalm 73:26 became my anchor: "My flesh and my heart may fail, but God is the strength of my heart and my portion forever." When doctors said 15%, Heaven declared 100%. My spirit found peace in God's promises, even when my body was weak.

The Real Battle Begins

We left the hospital in silence. Yet, as we pulled into the driveway, the Holy Spirit spoke clearly to my heart: "Now the real work begins. Now you will see what I can do when medicine meets its limit."

The medical verdict wasn't my defeat. It was my call to arms. If natural medicine could no longer heal me, then supernatural medicine would have to take over. If human wisdom had reached its limits, then divine wisdom would have to intervene.

Romans 4:20–21 speaks of Abraham: "He did not waver at the promise of God through unbelief, but was strengthened in faith, giving glory to God, being fully convinced that what He had promised He was also able to perform." I clung to that Word.

I understood that I had now entered uncharted territory, where faith would be my compass, God's Word my map, and the Holy Spirit my guide. The real battle was no longer being fought in a hospital room; it was being fought in the heavenly realm.

That moment of realization was holy. It didn't change the numbers on my medical chart, but it changed the narrative in my heart. Fear lifted; peace settled in. Isaiah 41:10 whispered to me, "Fear not, for I am with you; be not dismayed, for I am your God. I will strengthen you and help you." And Psalm 107:20 declared, "He sent His word and healed them, and delivered them from their destructions."

Divine Helpers Along the Way

God began using both natural and supernatural tools to rebuild me from the inside out.

A dear friend, a homeopathic specialist, suggested I try grounding—the practice of walking barefoot on the earth to restore the body's natural electrical balance. Research has shown that absorbing the earth's electrons can reduce inflammation, alleviate stress, and improve sleep. Every morning, I would step outside, barefoot on the cool ground, and pray, believing God could use the very earth He had created to help heal my broken heart.

Mary, the ARMI regional leader who had rallied the prayer support, stayed closely connected with me through constant prayer and practical encouragement. She suggested Moringa tea—an anti-inflammatory herbal remedy known for its rich nutritional value.

Moringa is packed with vitamins, minerals, and antioxidants, and it truly helped calm my system.

I believe God was using these resources—both the natural remedies suggested by friends and the spiritual wisdom available to me—as instruments of His total provision.

🔍 Reflection Prompts

What "final verdict" has been spoken over your life?

What percentage of hope have you been given?

Whatever it is, know that Heaven has the last Word. God specializes in turning a 15% hope into a 100% testimony.

🙏 Prayer Declaration

Lord, when human wisdom reaches its limit, Your infinite wisdom is just beginning. When medical options are exhausted, your supernatural options are limitless. I refuse to accept any diagnosis as final when you have the final Word. Transform my 15% into 100% – my impossible into the inevitable, my hopeless situation into a platform for the supernatural. I release fear and choose faith. I declare that my body, mind, and spirit are aligned with Your healing power. Let this verdict become the stage for your miraculous intervention. I choose victory over victimhood; I choose your report over any other. I declare life, healing, and resurrection power over my situation, in Jesus' name. Amen

⚡ Unshakable Charge

When the world pronounced a final verdict of defeat – a meager fifteen-percent chance of survival – Heaven's authority thundered with a greater decree: Life and victory in Jesus' name.

What others called the end; God called a new beginning. The medical report was not the final Word over your life; Almighty God's Word is the final authority. The Lord who spoke creation into existence has the last Word on your destiny, and He declares, "You shall not die, but live" (Psalm 118:17).

Take heart and stand firm. God's power is not limited by human prognosis. He is the Alpha and Omega, the First and the Last (Revelation 22:13) – no verdict stands above His. He promises, "I am the LORD who heals you" (Exodus 15:26), and by His stripes you are healed (Isaiah 53:5).

You are not a victim of circumstance – you are a victor through Christ. The same spirit that raised Jesus from the dead lives in you, breathing resurrection life into your mortal body (Romans 8:11). Through Him, you are more than a conqueror (Romans 8:37) – an overcomer armed with unshakable faith. So, reject every whisper of fear and every lie of the enemy, for God has not given you a spirit of fear, but of power, love, and a sound mind (2 Timothy 1:7).

Refuse to dwell in despair; refuse to settle for defeat. Lift your head and see with eyes of faith – Heaven's promise outweighs earth's prognosis.

Therefore, I charge you: stand boldly and cling to the Lord's unfailing Word as your ultimate truth. Trust the Great Physician above every earthly prognosis. Let your faith roar louder than fear. Let your life prove that no verdict of man can nullify the victory of God. Heaven has the last Word over your life, and His Word is final.

I refuse to fear. I choose faith. I rise empowered by His Word.

I am **UNSHAKABLE**

CHAPTER 8

THE ROAD TO FORGIVENESS

The Weapon I Almost Missed

There are many tools in the arsenal of spiritual healing—faith, declarations, worship, nutrition, rest—but none surprised me more than the one I had overlooked for so long: Forgiveness.

After receiving the devastating medical verdict—15% chance of survival, no option for bypass or stent surgery—I returned home not defeated but determined. The diagnosis may have been final in the natural realm, but I had access to a higher court. I resolved to fight on every level.

I pressed deeper into prayer. I surrounded myself with Scripture. I continued my healthy eating regimen while also exploring new natural remedies. A dear sister suggested "grounding"—the practice of walking barefoot on the earth to reconnect the body with the healing frequencies of nature.

But grounding was painful. My body was frail. The tiny twigs in my backyard pierced my feet, so I started driving to the soft grass near an elementary school a few blocks away. The physical discomfort was a constant reminder of my struggle. I walked barefoot in the early morning light, whispering prayers into the sky, begging Heaven for divine healing. I wasn't sure if it would work, but I kept walking, kept praying, and kept believing.

Then, one day, on my knees, I cried out: "Lord, I know what the doctors said. But what do You say?"

And He responded clearly, not with a new promise, but with a holy rebuke wrapped in love:

"Daughter, I will not change My Word for you. My Word is eternal. But I need you to align with My Word—in spirit, soul, and body."

But I realized that Forgiveness isn't just a spiritual act; it can also unlock physical healing. By forgiving, I was releasing the emotional toxins that hindered my body's recovery, showing that Forgiveness is vital for holistic health.

The Razor Blade Soup Dream

That night, I had a vivid dream. I was sitting at a table, holding a bowl of soup. It looked warm and comforting. But as I dipped my spoon in and lifted it toward my mouth, I noticed something horrifying—razor blades floating inside.

I jolted awake, shaken. Immediately, the Holy Spirit whispered:

"That is what bitterness looks like—it may seem nourishing, but every bite wounds you from the inside out."

Bitterness is poison that secretly harms your spirit and body, making it vital to recognize its destructive power.

The Scientific Truth Behind the Bitterness

Science reveals that Forgiveness is not merely a choice of faith, but a crucial mechanism for regulating your body's stress and healing processes. Unforgiveness causes genuine physiological harm. When you hold onto bitterness, your body enters a chronic state of stress known as the "fight or flight" response. This continuously floods your system with cortisol and adrenaline.

Dr. Caroline Leaf, a cognitive neuroscientist, explains the physical toll of toxic emotions:

"Toxic thoughts are real physiological entities that grow in your brain and stress your body, leading to ill health. Studies show that holding onto unforgiveness can increase inflammation and even weaken the immune system." (Source: Switch On Your Brain, Dr. Caroline Leaf, PhD)

This chronic stress directly impacts your cardiovascular and digestive systems, mirroring many of my symptoms:

Cardiovascular Strain: Holding a grudge elevates blood pressure and heart rate. A study published in the Journal of Behavioral Medicine found that individuals who practice Forgiveness show reduced cardiovascular activity in response to stress.

Immune Suppression: Chronic cortisol suppresses the immune system, making the body susceptible to inflammation and slower to heal. Researchers at Duke University Medical Center found a strong correlation between high hostility levels and poor cardiac outcomes.

The Scripture warned us clearly: "Get rid of all bitterness, rage and anger... forgiving each other, just as in Christ God forgave you." (Ephesians 4:31-32). This is God prescribing the ultimate treatment for emotional wellness.

I had forgiven loudly and publicly. I would tell people, "It's all good now." But God began to highlight one particular relationship—a relative who had betrayed my trust, wounded me deeply, and left scars I thought I'd buried. I hadn't truly forgiven. I had locked them out of my heart to protect myself. But in doing so, I had locked myself into a prison of pain.

"What if they hurt me again?" I asked God, feeling vulnerable. He gently replied, "Forgiveness is about freeing yourself, not about trusting blindly. It's a process of healing that allows you to move forward without carrying the burden of bitterness."

"Forgiveness doesn't mean forgetting or excusing the hurt," He explained. "It begins with choosing to release the pain, praying for their healing, and surrendering the offense to God. Start by praying for the person who hurt you, and ask God to help you let go of bitterness."

Additional Scripture for the Mind-Body Connection

The Bible repeatedly confirms the connection between spiritual peace and physical health:

"A heart at peace gives life to the body, but envy rots the bones." — Proverbs 14:30 (NIV)

"Is anyone among you sick? Let him call for the elders of the church... and the prayer of faith will save the one who is sick, and the Lord will raise him up, and if he has committed sins, he will be forgiven." — James 5:14-15 (ESV)

"But if you do not forgive others their trespasses, neither will your Father forgive your trespasses." — Matthew 6:15 (ESV)

The Prophetic Foot Washing (Breaking the Chains)

Years earlier, I had another dream in which Prophet Robyn Vincent washed my feet, which were caked in thick mud. I tucked it away, unsure of its meaning. Seven years later, that dream came true.

Robyn, a fellow member at Glory of Zion, invited me to a prophetic foot-washing event. I was so weak I couldn't even drive. But something inside me said I had to go. I ordered an Uber and arrived late, breathless and inflamed, unsure if I could even walk in.

By the time I entered, the foot washing was already in progress. I noticed each woman had one person washing her feet. But when it was my turn, something extraordinary happened: five women surrounded me. I was seated, trembling, struggling to breathe. They knelt in tears and began to wash my swollen feet, praying with authority and compassion. I felt the Lord's compassion in that holy moment.

The prayers were bold: "Lord, heal what no medicine can reach. Break every chain, every soul tie, every root of bitterness. Wash her past, her pain, her prison."

I wept uncontrollably. These women were living extensions of Jesus. At that moment, the chains broke. The bitterness left. And the miraculous healing began to flow freely again.

What I Didn't Realize

I had been using all the tools—scriptures, nutrition, supplements, grounding, declarations—but none could override the toxic effects of unforgiveness. Unforgiveness was the silent barrier—the dam that blocked the river of healing.

I had to forgive:

People who misunderstood me.

Anyone who judged my faith.

Those who ghosted me in my suffering.

And myself, for getting sick, for missing signs, for being unable to fix everything.

Healing is not just about medication or miracles—it's also about obedience and alignment. God said, "I love you, but I won't override My own Word." Forgiveness was my necessary act of alignment.

Practical Steps to Forgiveness

If you're reading this and struggling with Forgiveness, you're not alone. Practical steps can help you move forward. Here are some actions I took that might empower you too:

Step Action

1. Name the Pain Be honest about who hurt you and how it affected you.
2. Write a Release Letter Pour it out onto paper (you don't have to send it).
3. Speak the Release Forgiveness is more powerful when declared aloud.
4. Ask for Strength Forgiveness is a supernatural act—it often requires divine intervention.
5. Let It Be Ongoing Forgiveness is a journey. You may need to reaffirm it more than once.

🔍 Reflection Prompts

Are You Eating Razor-Blade Soup?

Are you consuming something that looks comforting but is slowly wounding your soul?

Bitterness may feel safe, but it is a spiritual toxin. Unforgiveness might feel justified, but it becomes a chain around your own freedom.

Who do you need to forgive today? A parent? A partner? A church leader? Yourself? Ask the Holy Spirit to show you. He is gentle but thorough. Your breakthrough may be waiting on the other side of that release.

🕊 Healing Scriptures

"Praise the Lord, my soul, and forget not all his benefits—who forgives all your sins and heals all your diseases." —Psalm 103:2–3

"Be kind and compassionate to one another, forgiving each other, just as in Christ God forgave you." —Ephesians 4:32

🙏 Prayer Declaration

Lord, search every corner of my heart. Shine your light on any hidden places where bitterness and unforgiveness are still hiding. I release every offense, every betrayal, every disappointment; past and present. I choose freedom. I choose mercy. I choose to heal. Remove every root of resentment, and let Your river of life flow through my Spirit, soul, and body. Thank you for the strength to forgive; and for forgiving me. In Jesus' name, Amen

⚡ Unshakable Charge

Forgiveness isn't a feeling; it's a faith act.

You are not weak for letting go. You are strong for choosing healing.

Today, choose freedom over fury. Peace over punishment. Healing over holding on.

The cross has already paid for it all. Don't let bitterness rob you of the healing that belongs to you, the complete and transformative healing that forgiveness brings.

Walk barefoot into God's presence and let Him wash your wounds with mercy.

You are not just recovering.

You are rising—**UNSHAKABLE.**

CHAPTER 9

THE UNSEEN HAND

When Grace Met Me At Costco

I woke up that morning carrying the crushing weight I had for months—a 15% survival verdict pronounced by my doctors. It loomed like a dark cloud. Yet even beneath its heaviness, I clung to a higher truth: each sunrise was a divine invitation to declare life.

After my morning devotion, I whispered, "Lord, who would You have me intercede for today?" Despite the death sentence hanging over me, I wanted to remain useful in the Kingdom. I longed to pray for someone else's breakthrough even as I waited for my own.

Later that day, I gathered enough strength to make a trip to Costco. Every outing took immense courage, but I would not let sickness strip me of all I loved.

I paused at a demo table featuring turmeric and CoQ10. Curious, I struck up a conversation with the woman behind the table and casually said, "I'm here with a 15% life verdict. Just looking for something that might help."

Without hesitation, she reached across the table and prayed for me, reminding me that divine interruptions can come unexpectedly to strengthen our faith and keep us focused on God's presence in trials.

As I made my way toward the register, a young woman approached. She was full of light and warmth.

"Excuse me," she said gently, "I don't mean to be weird, but the Lord just pointed you out to me. I'm supposed to pray for you."

Her name was Grace.

Only hours earlier, I had asked the Lord to show me who I was supposed to pray for, and God flipped the script, encouraging me to trust His divine plan even when it surprises us.

We stood in the middle of Costco, holding hands, tears streaming, prayers flowing. Carts buzzed around us. Shoppers passed by unaware. But in that moment, Aisle 5 became a sanctuary. Heaven had come close.

Houston: A Divine Appointment

A few weeks later, I made the courageous decision to attend a ministry partner breakfast in Houston, hosted by Christ for All Nations (CFAN), known for its global crusades.

I had been a faithful partner for years. I weighed 109 pounds. My strength was fading, but my faith was fierce, a declaration of my divine destiny—I had to be there.

As I entered the venue, a familiar face approached me hesitantly. A dear prayer partner stared at my name tag. "Are you… Cathy?" she asked. She didn't recognize me. The look on her face said it all. My physical appearance had changed so much—yet in her shock, she wrapped me in love and prayed over me with a fierce tenderness.

Later that morning, as I stood quietly in the crowd, Evangelist Kolenda walked over and gently laid his hand on me.

He didn't know my full story. But Heaven did.

The moment he prayed, something shifted. I felt it deep within— the heat of the Holy Spirit surging through my body, bypassing logic, penetrating pain.

I didn't need fanfare. I needed fire. And I received it.

On the bus ride home, I was still physically weak. But my spirit soared. I sang softly under my breath. Healing was not just happening in my body—it was unfolding in my soul.

Walmart: Another Messenger Sent

One ordinary day, I went to Walmart to pick up a few items. As I was leaving, a young woman with a gentle smile and a comforting presence approached me.

"I don't know what you're going through," she whispered, "but God told me to tell you—He sees you. He's not finished with you."

Then she prayed. Boldly. Fiercely. Prophetic fire flowed from her lips. I stood still, soaking it in.

The same unmistakable presence I had felt at Costco and in Houston met me again at Walmart.

Three places. Three women. Three divine appointments. Each one, a lifeline from Heaven.

Entertaining Angels Unaware

Scripture says in Hebrews 13:2, "Do not forget to show hospitality to strangers, for by so doing some have entertained angels without knowing it."

Were these women angels? I may never know.

But I know this: each one was sent by God.

Grace, the demo lady, and the woman at Walmart were more than kind souls; they were divine messengers sent by God to remind me I am seen, held, and fought for in His rescue mission.

When the Enemy Whispers

Not all battles are loud. Some are whispered.

Each morning, I woke to a taunting voice: "You won't make it. What's the point? Just give up."

But I remembered Deuteronomy 30:19: "I have set before you life and death, blessings and curses. Now choose life..."

So, I chose life.

Every. Single. Day.

I whispered Psalm 118:17: "I shall not die, but live, and declare the works of the Lord."

I let life-giving words echo louder than death's threats.

Reflection Prompts

Are you slowing down enough to notice the people God sends your way?

Can you recognize divine interruptions, even in ordinary places?

Are you willing to receive ministry even while you're still waiting on your own miracle?

Has God used strangers to speak life into your journey?

Let this chapter remind you: God is never out of messengers. You are never out of reach. And your healing journey is not a solo mission.

Healing Scriptures

Do not forget to show hospitality to strangers, for by so doing some people have entertained angels without knowing it." — Hebrews 13:2

"I have set before your life and death... Now choose life." — Deuteronomy 30:19

"I shall not die, but live, and declare the works of the Lord." — Psalm 118:17

"The Lord is near to the brokenhearted and saves the crushed in Spirit." — Psalm 34:18

"Fear not, for I am with you... I will uphold you with my righteous right hand." — Isaiah 41:10

Prayer Declaration

Father, I thank You for the unseen hand guiding me through dark valleys. Thank you for every divine encounter, every stranger who became an angel, and every moment when Your presence broke through my pain. Today, I choose life. I silence every whisper of fear, discouragement, and despair. Let your voice be the loudest in my heart. Help me see the Grace You send, and help me be Grace to others. My story is not over. I will live to declare Your goodness. In Jesus' name, Amen.

🙏 Prayer Declaration

You may be walking through what feels like a death sentence, but don't hand the enemy the pen. You have a role in how this chapter ends. You are not forgotten. You are not forsaken. You are not finished. Just as God sent Grace to me at Costco, He is sending help to you. And just as He sent me messengers, He will send you to be one with Him. So, rise, frail body, shaken faith, weary heart and all. You are Heaven's warrior in aisle 5. God's glory is about to break out in the most unexpected places. Hold on. Heaven is closer than you think.

You are **UNSHAKABLE.**

CHAPTER 10

MANTLED IN GOLD

The Divine Exchange That Marked My Turning Point

The journey that began with those unexpected divine encounters led me to a sacred moment that would forever change how I viewed my healing process. I discovered that healing was never just about my heart muscle. It was about the mantle God was preparing to place upon me. And sometimes, the turning point in your healing journey doesn't come in a hospital room. It comes in the most unexpected and hopeful places, like a simple supper with women of faith during Passover.

After months of being confined to a strict health regimen and barely having the strength to attend anything beyond necessary appointments, I had all but written off attending in-person gatherings. But something stirred in me when I received the invitation to attend the Women's House of Zion (WHOZ) Supper during Passover at Glory of Zion.

Understanding Passover

For readers unfamiliar with this biblical observance: Passover is a biblical feast that commemorates God's deliverance of the Israelites from Egyptian bondage (Exodus 12). God commanded Israel to mark their doors with the blood of a lamb so the angel of death would 'pass over' their homes. "The blood will be a sign for you on the houses where you are, and when I see the blood, I will pass over you." (Exodus 12:13) For Christians, it is a powerful foreshadowing of Christ, the Lamb of God, whose blood protects and delivers. Participating in Passover isn't about religion. It's about recognizing that the same God who delivered Israel still delivers today.

It was a daunting prospect, considering my health challenges and the considerable distance from my home, but I felt a compelling nudge to go.

It wasn't just a meal. It was a sacred appointment, a transformative moment. Hosted by Apostle Diana Lookabough, this annual event was always filled with prophetic worship, connection, and fresh oil for the women leading Houses of Zion. I had planned to just watch it online; the idea of being there in person, especially with my health challenges, felt like a daunting task. I hadn't been to Glory of Zion in over six months.

But something, no someone nudged me. Go.

Obedience in Weakness

I obeyed. Not because I had the strength, but because I sensed something was waiting for me on the other side of my obedience. This is often how faith works. We walk not by how we feel but by where we're led. It's not about feeling strong or capable but about trusting that there's a purpose in our actions, even when we're at our weakest.

I didn't go expecting anything. I just wanted to be in the room. I sat quietly at the table, frail in body, still trying to gain weight, still battling symptoms. I could barely eat anything because of my strict dietary limitations: no gluten, sugar, preservatives, or inflammatory foods. But being in that atmosphere with other women of faith was food to my soul.

Then something sacred happened.

The Golden Exchange

As I sat at the table, Fran, one of the leaders and a dear sister in the Lord, approached me gently. Without saying a word, she knelt beside me and draped a gold mantle over my shoulders.

Tears welled up in my eyes.

She had no idea what this meant to me. Months earlier, I had been fitted with a heart defibrillator vest, a visible reminder that my heart was failing. Doctors wanted to implant a pacemaker, a permanent device that would keep my heart from stopping. I had declined.

This mantle represented something more profound than fabric. It was a divine exchange. In that moment, I felt Heaven say: "You will not be marked by machinery. You are marked by Me."

The gold was not just a color. It was a symbol of wealth and power. In the Bible, gold represents divinity, kingship, purity, and the presence of God. Priests wore gold in the tabernacle. The ark of the covenant was overlaid in gold. Gold speaks of glory.

That night, I was being mantled with glory, not weakness. I wasn't just recovering; I was being commissioned. God was clothing me with purpose, even in the middle of my pain. This was my divine commissioning.

"...to appoint unto them that mourn in Zion, to give unto them beauty for ashes, the oil of joy for mourning, the garment of praise for the spirit of heaviness..." (Isaiah 61:3)

What Is a Mantle?

For those unfamiliar with biblical language, a mantle was a prophet's garment that symbolized calling, authority, and divine assignment. When Elijah passed his mantle to Elisha, it marked a transfer of spiritual inheritance and mission (2 Kings 2:13-15).

In modern terms, being mantled means being clothed with a divine mandate. It's like being given a special mission or purpose that you couldn't accomplish on your own. You are marked for an assignment beyond your ability, an assignment that only God can empower you to fulfill.

This divine mantle is not just a piece of fabric, but a symbol of God's authority and power in your life, a clear sign of your divine destiny.

The Weight of Glory vs. the Weight of Diagnosis

I left that night not with fear of my failing heart but with fresh faith in a faithful God. I came into that room with weakness draped over me, but I left with glory wrapped around me.

What pacemaker could match that?

This divine moment reminded me that God doesn't just heal us to make us comfortable. He heals us to commission us. He restores so that He can release. The weight of a gold mantle replaced the weight of diagnosis in my life. I experienced a personal exodus from fear to faith, from affliction to assignment.

"Now the Lord is the Spirit, and where the Spirit of the Lord is, there is liberty." (2 Corinthians 3:17)

From Survivor to Messenger

This experience was more than just healing; it was a form of preparation for the next chapter of my life. I came to understand that I hadn't merely survived something medically remarkable. I had entered into a divine storyline, one crafted by God Himself.

This narrative is not only about my physical healing but also about the purpose and mission God has for my life. It reflects how He wants to use my experiences to encourage and inspire others.

And so have you.

You may be reading this with a diagnosis over your life, or with deep discouragement clouding your future. But I believe the same God who mantled me with gold is preparing to mantle you. You are being wrapped in purpose. Covered in promise. Cloaked in calling.

Don't give up. Your exchange is coming.

🔍 Reflection Prompts

Have you ever overlooked a sacred invitation because of physical or emotional limitations?

What if your obedience to attend is the very act that releases your breakthrough?

Are you willing to trade in your garment of heaviness for a mantle of glory?

Take time to ask God if there's an invitation you've ignored because you didn't feel strong enough to accept it. He may be calling you to a divine appointment that will change everything.

📜 Healing Scriptures

"Arise, shine, for your light has come, and the glory of the Lord rises upon you." Isaiah 60:1

"To give them beauty for ashes, the oil of joy for mourning, the garment of praise for the spirit of heaviness." Isaiah 61:3

"Now the Lord is the Spirit, and where the Spirit of the Lord is, there is liberty." 2 Corinthians 3:17

The mantle of Elijah that fell from him... Now when the sons of the prophets who were from Jericho saw him, they said, "The spirit of Elijah rests on Elisha." 2 Kings 2:13-15

🙏 Prayer Declaration

Father, thank You for divine exchanges. Thank You for showing me that I am not defined by my diagnosis, but by Your promise. I trade every garment of fear, shame, and weakness for the mantle of glory You've prepared for me. Clothe me with purpose. Wrap me in healing. Anoint me to rise stronger, wiser, and fully mantled for my assignment. In Jesus' name, Amen.

⚡ Unshakable Charge

I am not just recovering. I am rising. I am not marked by diagnosis. I am mantled by destiny. I will walk boldly in the calling God has placed on my life, clothed in His power and wrapped in His glory. My healing is not just for survival. It's for assignment.

I am **UNSHAKABLE.**

CHAPTER 11

WELCOME TO THE LAND
OF THE LIVING

When Faith Burns the Funeral Clothes

I woke up with tears streaming down my face, overwhelmed by God's divine healing and resurrection power that overturned every earthly diagnosis.

In the dream, I was in my backyard, digging into the earth with fierce determination, symbolizing my faith's fight against spiritual death and despair, inspiring hope in the unseen power of God.

These were the funeral clothes the enemy had tried to wrap around my calling.

With authority I didn't know I possessed, I gathered those sticks and lit them on fire, symbolizing God's burning away every lie and limitation. The flames rose like incense, consuming every negative label the world had put on me.

Suddenly, the scene changed. I stood at the start of a race track, surrounded by the great cloud of witnesses described in Hebrews 12:1. Their eyes were fixed on me, not in judgment, but in fierce encouragement.

I wasn't crawling. I wasn't limping. I was sprinting.

With every stride, I ran past trauma. I outran fatigue. I shattered every barrier that once tried to define me. As I crossed the finish line, I was handed a trophy—a weighty, golden crown of honor, adorned with jewels that sparkled in the sunlight.

It wasn't just a race—it was a divine resurrection.

Then I heard the whisper of the Holy Spirit: "Welcome to the Land of the Living."

I woke up breathless. Healed. Whole. Alive in every sense of the word.

Resurrection Before The Report

By Easter weekend 2024, a profound transformation had taken place. It was Resurrection Sunday—how fitting. And for the first time in over a year, I stood in front of a crowd—not as a patient, not as a prayer request—but as a praiser, a living testament to the power of supernatural healing.

I had been invited to join the choir for all three Easter services. Months earlier, walking from my bedroom to the bathroom left me gasping for air. Now, I was standing on stage—singing, worshiping, dancing. The same lungs that once struggled to breathe were now lifting praises to the King of Kings.

I ate a full sandwich for the first time in over a year: no pain, no nausea, no bloating. I laughed with friends and wept tears of joy. My body was recovering, yes—but more importantly, my soul had been resurrected.

I didn't need a doctor's report to believe it—Heaven's promise had already confirmed my hope, encouraging you to declare God's promises over your life.

The Medical Confirmation

In August 2024, I underwent a comprehensive cardiac workup, which included an MRI, EKG, stress test, and echocardiogram.

The technicians reviewed the scans and then paused. They whispered. They ran the test again. Then again.

"This doesn't match your previous charts," one said, confused.

I watched their faces shift from confusion to amazement. It was the third time they had restarted the test. This wasn't the heart of someone who survived death. This heart was alive, strong, and pumping with divine vitality.

A few weeks later, the official call came.

"Ms. Ogie, your heart is no longer diseased."

There it was—Heaven's report confirmed on paper. The grave clothes had been burned. The 'RIP' prophecy had been reversed. My identity had been rewritten from terminal to triumphant.

A Doctor's Amazement

In February 2025, I had my six-month cardiology checkup.

My cardiologist, who had walked with me through the darkest valleys, stared at me with wide-eyed wonder.

"I was about to remind you about your bypass surgery," he said, smiling. "But clearly... you won't be needing one."

He had no words. But he didn't need them. What science couldn't explain, Scripture had already declared.

Ezekiel 37:5 – "This is what the Sovereign Lord says to these bones: I will make breath enter you, and you will come to life."

I didn't just survive. I was resurrected.

From RIP to Risen

That dream was more than imagery; it was spiritual warfare, with burning RIP sticks symbolizing victory over death and despair, reinforcing divine authority over life and death.

When I ran that race, I was stepping into my calling. At the finish line, holding the trophy, I received divine restoration.

God didn't just repair what was broken. He revived what was buried.

The journey wasn't instant. It came in layers: A whisper. A worship. A dream. A report. A race. A radical resurrection.

Don't Bury Yourself Too Soon

Dear reader, perhaps you've received a report that took your breath away. Perhaps a diagnosis has led you to question your destiny. But let me lovingly declare: Don't bury yourself too soon.

Psalm 118:17 says, "I shall not die, but live, and declare the works of the Lord."

You are not finished. The Author of your story is not done writing.

Isaiah 53:1 asks: "Who has believed our report? And to whom has the arm of the Lord been revealed?"

God is inviting you to believe His report today.

Resurrection always starts with a choice: A choice to believe. A choice to hope again. A choice to set fire to what the enemy said would define you.

🔍 Reflection Prompts

What labels have you buried that still need to be burned?

What RIP verdicts have you agreed with out of fear or fatigue?

Where is God whispering, "Arise, my child"?

Are you still waiting on man's confirmation—or are you living by Heaven's decree?

🕊 Healing Scriptures

Psalm 118:17 – "I shall not die, but live, and declare the works of the Lord."

Ezekiel 37:6 – "I will put breath in you, and you will come to life."

Isaia 40:31 – "But they that wait upon the Lord shall renew their strength…"

John 11:25 – "I am the Resurrection and the life. He who believes in Me will live, even though he dies."

Malachi 4:2 – "But for you who fear my name, the Sun of Righteousness will rise with healing in His wings."

🙏 Prayer Declaration

Father, I thank You that You are the God who brings the dead back to life. 1 release every diagnosis, every fear, every label that tried to define me. I declare: I shall not die but live, and I will declare Your mighty works. I choose to walk in faith, to burn the funeral clothes, and to believe Your report. Thank you for resurrecting my body, restoring my Spirit, and redeeming my time. In Jesus' name, Amen.

⚡ Unshakable Charge

Today, I choose life. I choose to reject every report that doesn't align with Heaven's decree. I burn the funeral clothes, silence the grave whisper, and rise with fresh fire. I am not a victim—I am a victor. I am not what I was—I am who God says I am. I live, move, and breathe in resurrection power. This is not the end. This is the land of the living.

I am **UNSHAKABLE.**

CHAPTER 12

SONGS IN THE NIGHT

WHEN HEAVEN SINGS OVER THE BROKEN

Some healings come in an instant. Others, like mine, come like the dawn—slow, quiet, almost imperceptible, yet unmistakably sure. In the silence of my darkest nights, I learned to listen, not just for answers or a change in diagnosis, but for the transformative songs God was singing over me. This was my journey of worship healing.

Psalm 42:8 says, "By day the Lord directs his love, at night his song is with me—a prayer to the God of my life."

This verse became a lifeline. It was not just poetic; it was my reality. While my body was deteriorating, while doctors scratched their heads and my loved ones whispered prayers in hospital corridors, the Holy Spirit would descend with melodies that no radio could play and no worship team could compose.

The Midnight Melodies

There were nights when I couldn't sleep. The weight of my body felt foreign, like I was trapped inside a cage of fatigue and pain. My stomach could not hold food. I experienced an irregular heartbeat. My breath came shallow. Yet in that fragility, something sacred would stir.

One night, around 3 AM, as the monitors blinked and beeped rhythmically beside my hospital bed, I heard it—a soft tune. At first, I thought a nurse had left the TV on, but no. The melody was not external. It was internal, divine, a love song whispered from Heaven directly into my soul. I found myself humming along, tears falling silently, my spirit wrapped in what I can only describe as liquid hope. The Great Physician was not just healing me; He was serenading me with a divine melody of hope that can also uplift you in your suffering.

Zephaniah 3:17 came alive: "The Lord your God is with you, the Mighty Warrior who saves. He will take great delight in you; in his love he will no longer rebuke you, but will rejoice over you with singing."

I was not alone.

Night Songs and the War for Hope

There were several nights like that. Nights when the pain was too much, and yet, instead of despair, I felt the atmosphere shift. A new song would be deposited in my heart—sometimes just a phrase, sometimes a full chorus.

I would scribble them into the notes section of my phone, not knowing then that they were more than lullabies. They were spiritual weapons.

In Job 35:10, Elihu says, 'But no one says, "Where is God my Maker, who gives songs in the night?"' I began actively seeking that question, not out of accusation but out of expectation. 'Lord, what song are you singing tonight?' I encourage you to ask the same-listen for His divine melodies in your night seasons, trusting He will answer with hope and reassurance.

And He would answer.

One night, I heard: "There is healing in My breath, restoration in My gaze. Trust Me through the valley; I will renew your days." I wept.

Another night: "You are not forgotten, not left behind. My promises are tethered to you like vines. I will raise you, replant you, revive you, and cause you to bloom in time."

Each time, I would feel a surge of hope. The kind that doctors can't prescribe. The kind that breaks chains deep in the soul.

Holy Downloads and Healing Through Worship

Worship became more than music; it was a form of spiritual medicine. Not the kind taken orally, but the kind that renews your soul. Sometimes I couldn't speak because of weakness, but I would play instrumental worship and let it wash over me, bringing healing and renewal to my spirit.

These weren't always well-known songs. Often, they were spontaneous, heavenly downloads. I believe God was speaking to me, bypassing my intellect and ministering directly to my spirit.

Psalm 77:6 says, "I remembered my songs in the night. My heart meditated and my spirit asked." That became my pattern. The night became my sanctuary. My bed, an altar. My breath, a prayer.

I would wake up with lyrics rolling off my tongue. Sometimes the song would be a declaration of healing. Other times, it would be a gentle reminder that I was not alone.

Once, during a particularly low point when my blood pressure had dropped dangerously, I heard this phrase repeat in my heart: "I am the God who sees, the One who stays. Even when your body fades, I remain." My fingers trembled, but I typed it anyway. Because every song carried healing. And I wanted to remember.

A Diary of Divine Lullabies

Here are some lines I recorded over those months. They may not rhyme or follow musical structure, but they were sacred. Perhaps one of them is meant for you:

"I will carry you through the shadows, for I walk in them, too."

"In your silence, I am speaking louder than pain."

"Your dry bones will sing again."

"The fire didn't consume you; it anointed you."

"I have numbered your nights; none are wasted."

God's songs are not just melodies, but messages of hope and strength. They lifted my head when I could not lift my hands. They reminded me that I was not forgotten. Not forsaken. Not beyond repair.

The Song That Wrote Me Back to Life

Eventually, I began to sing again. Not just hum, but sing out loud, weakly at first, like a newborn learning to cry. Then louder. Then boldly. My vocal cords had not been used in weeks, but as I sang, I felt a surge of strength rise within me.

Healing did not come all at once. But the songs kept coming, and I kept listening, singing, and believing.

And then one day, I felt like the song inside me had changed. It wasn't just a song of survival. It was a song of resurrection.

I remember that morning. I had just finished whispering a prayer when a new melody came: "You have walked through fire, but not alone. You wear my glory; you are My own."

I sang it again and again. And in that moment, I felt the Spirit of God rise up inside me, stronger than the symptoms, louder than the diagnosis.

This was more than music. It was a rebirth.

Why the Night Matters

Friend, if you find yourself in the night season—waiting, wondering, weeping—know this: The God who made you has a song for you, too. He is not silent. He does not slumber. He is rejoicing over you with singing.

Lean in.

Ask Him, "What are You singing tonight?"

You may not get a full song. You may get a phrase, a picture, or a hum in your spirit. Write it down. Sing it back to Him. Let it become your anthem.

For some, healing will look like a clean bill of health. For others, it will be the unshakable courage to face the next day. Either way, your healing is wrapped in the intimacy of His presence.

He still sings songs in the night.

And if you listen closely—past the fear, past the pain, past the noise of this world—you will hear Him singing over you, too.

Your midnight is not the end of your story. It is the beginning of your most beautiful song.

Listen. Receive. Sing back.

For the God who composed the stars also composes melodies of hope in the hearts of His children.

And your song? It has already begun.

🔍 Reflection Prompts

Have you ever heard God speak through music or melody?

What song has helped you through a difficult season?

Ask the Lord to give you a song in your night. What do you hear?

🕊 Healing Scriptures

"By day the Lord directs his love, at night his song is with me—a prayer to the God of my life." —Psalm 42:8

"The Lord your God is in your midst, a mighty one who will save; He will rejoice over you with gladness; He will quiet you by his love; He will exult over you with loud singing." —Zephaniah 3:17

"I remembered my songs in the night. My heart meditated and my spirit asked." —Psalm 77:6

"He gives songs in the night." —Job 35:10

"Sing to the Lord, you His faithful ones, and praise His holy name. For His anger lasts only a moment, but His favor, a lifetime. Weeping may endure for a night, but joy comes in the morning." —Psalm 30:4

🙏 Prayer Declaration

Father, I thank You that You are not silent in my night. You are singing over me, even when I feel alone. I declare that I will hear Your voice through the darkness. I receive the songs you are depositing into my Spirit. Let every melody break chains, bring healing, and restore my hope. I declare that you are my song and my salvation. I will praise You in the midnight hour, for I know joy comes in the morning. Amen.

⚡ Unshakable Charge

Rise, beloved. You are not forsaken in the silence. You are not forgotten in the shadows. There is a melody being written in your midnight that will carry you into morning. Do not lose heart. May the songs in your night be anthems of faith, not fear. Let worship be your war cry. Allow intimacy with God to anchor your soul. Let His whispers reshape your reality. You are not waiting in vain—He is weaving something holy in the hush. Walk through the valley with confidence, knowing that the One who sings over you also walks beside you. This is not the end. This is your becoming.

This is the sound of **UNSHAKABLE** faith.

EPILOGUE

Living Unshakable in a World of Shaking

You were never meant to live small.

Not silenced by trauma. Not shattered by diagnosis. You are not diminished by what you've survived.

You were born for the fire. Not the fire that consumes, but the fire that refines. The fire that awakens something dormant in your DNA. The fire that marks you for assignments greater than the pain you've endured.

If you're holding this book, it's not by accident. You are a survivor. A warrior. A living, breathing testimony that divine empowerment is available through prayer, faith, surrender, and actively seeking God's presence.

The Journey We've Walked Together

Throughout these chapters, we've journeyed through darkness and into light. We've wept together in emergency rooms, prayed together in midnight hours, and stood on trembling legs as healing broke through—layer by layer, moment by moment, miracle by miracle.

After facing a 15% survival verdict, you've watched me rise to 100% testimony. You've witnessed divine appointments in grocery store aisles and prophetic mantles at Passover dinners. You've heard the songs God sang over my brokenness and seen how those midnight melodies became morning declarations.

But now, as you close these pages, I want to leave you with something more than remembrance.

I want to hand you a mantle. A commissioning. A charge that will outlast the emotions this book stirred and anchor itself in the bedrock of who you're becoming.

Your Scars Are Your Sending

There is no shame in what you've endured.

The trauma. The surgical procedures. The uncertainty. The isolation. The treatments that failed. Prayers that appeared unanswered. The nights when death whispered your name.

None of it was wasted. All of it was sacred preparation.

Your scars are not signs of defeat. They are medals of survival,

"When you walk through the fire, you will not be burned; the flames will not set you ablaze." —Isaiah 43:2

You didn't just walk through. You came out with revelation. With resurrection power. With authority forged in the furnace.

The fire was your classroom. And now you carry healing embers in your hands. You are a carrier of hope and purpose, whether you feel qualified or not, because God's calling remains even in your pain.

Healing Is Not A Destination. It's a Lifestyle

If you're still waiting on healing, let me tell you what I learned through midnight songs and morning mercies:

Healing doesn't always arrive as a thunderclap.

Sometimes it trickles in on worship notes. Sometimes it hides in the obedience of drinking more water, changing your diet, forgiving the person who wounded you, or lying still long enough for God to breathe peace into your chaos.

Healing is layered. Often disguised in mundane moments. New habits, fresh faith, transformed language.

One of the greatest revelations I received on this journey: Healing is both a promise and a continuous process, encouraging patience and hope.

Just because the pain hasn't vanished doesn't mean the power isn't working. Just because you haven't crossed the finish line doesn't mean you're not making progress.

"He who began a good work in you will carry it on to completion until the day of Christ Jesus." —Philippians 1:6

Don't curse your process. Celebrate your progress.

Every breath is a victory. Every strengthened heartbeat is proof. Your testimony is written in real time with every step forward.

When doctors gave me 15% survival odds, I could have surrendered to despair.

When my organs began failing, I could have agreed with the medical reports. I could have let fear write my final chapter as people retreated, and isolation threatened to suffocate hope.

But God had other plans.

Like Joseph, I can now say with full confidence:

"You intended to harm me, but God intended it for good to accomplish what is now being done, the saving of many lives." — Genesis 50:20

This book is not just about my healing—it's about yours.

My fire birthed your invitation. My pain became a platform. And now I'm handing the microphone to you.

Rise, Warrior Of God

The enemy tried to silence your voice, but God is restoring your sound.

Trauma tried to shatter your identity, but the cross reclaims your name.

Illness tried to crush your joy, but Christ's resurrection renews your spirit.

You are not forgotten. You are not too broken. You are not too late.

You are the very one God chose to rise in this hour with a testimony forged in the furnace. You carry the aroma of survival. You bear the weight of glory.

"I consider that our present sufferings are not worth comparing with the glory that will be revealed in us." —Romans 8:18

Let your voice be loud. Let your prayers shake foundations. Let your life proclaim what your lips may still struggle to declare:

He still heals. He still speaks. He still raises the dead.

A Prophetic Declaration Over You

Listen closely. These are not empty words—they are prophetic decrees over your life:

You shall live and not die.

You shall see the goodness of the Lord in the land of the living.

Your latter days shall be greater than your former.

Every cell in your body is aligning with Heaven's blueprint. Your mind is being renewed with the truth that overpowers every lie. Your peace is returning like floodwaters breaking through drought. Your joy is being made full, not with superficial happiness, but with supernatural strength.

Your identity is no longer rooted in what happened to you. It's anchored in the unshakable love of Jesus Christ.

You are being clothed in boldness. Wrapped in healing. Mantled in holiness.

You will walk through hospital corridors not as a patient, but as a vessel of power.

You will speak life over your children, your community, your future.

The fear that once imprisoned you has become your launching pad into destiny.

The grave clothes are coming off. Weeping is turning to dancing.

The fire that nearly destroyed you is now your fuel for assignments you haven't imagined.

FINAL BLESSING

Beloved reader, may you live boldly.

You've walked with me from the edge of death to the gates of glory, through diagnoses, despair, and divine encounters. And now, as you turn this final page, I don't just want to say goodbye—I want to send you out with power, purpose, and prophetic fire.

This is not the end of the story. It's the beginning of yours.

You may be holding this book from a hospital bed, a waiting room, or a weary place where you've whispered prayers in the dark. Maybe you've wept quietly, wondering if God sees you. Perhaps you're worn out, and your soul is weary from holding onto beliefs.

But I'm here to tell you with everything in me: You are not forgotten. You are not forsaken. You are not finished.

You were never meant to die in the waiting room. You were never meant to drown in your diagnosis. You were never created to live buried under fear, shame, or exhaustion.

You were made for fire. You were made for healing. You were made to rise.

Heaven still has something to say about your story.

God is not just watching your battle from a distance—He is fighting with you. He's the one who holds your hand through every scan, who sits with you through every sleepless night, who catches every tear and bottles them as worship. Even when the world doesn't understand your pain, He does. And not only does He understand, He redeems.

In this moment, I declare over you a divine reversal:

What was meant for evil, God is already turning for your good (Genesis 50:20).

What looked like the end is only the setup for a miracle.

It may have felt like a delay, but it has been divine preparation.

If you've been waiting on your healing—body, mind, or spirit—I speak this truth into your soul: You are already seen. Already chosen. Already deeply loved.

This Is Your Charge

Let every scar on your body, every whisper of faith in the darkness, and every trembling prayer be a banner of victory. You are not broken—you are being rebuilt. You are not defeated—you are being refined. And your survival is not just for you. It's for those who will follow your light back to the foot of the cross.

You are marked for glory.

I bless you now with unshakable hope, undeniable strength, and unrelenting faith.

I bless your hands to war and win.

I bless your feet to walk purposefully into every promise.

I bless your voice to declare healing and freedom.

I bless your nights with rest and your days with joy.

I bless your body with divine recovery.

I bless your heart with the peace of Christ.

I bless your spirit to know deeply that you are loved beyond comprehension.

May the fire of revival burn within you—not a flicker, but a wildfire.

Let your testimony be a trumpet to awaken others.

May your tears become oil for someone else's healing.

You are unshakable, not because of your strength, but because of His.

And if you ever forget how far you've come, open this book again and remember:

The same God who raised Lazarus from the dead, who healed the bleeding woman, who walked through locked doors and broke every curse—He lives in you.

This is your commissioning moment.

It's time to walk like the healed.

To speak like the restored.

To worship like the delivered.

To live like the beloved.

You are a living miracle. You are proof that the resurrection is not a story—it's a Spirit. And that Spirit lives in you.

Now go—

Live like someone who has touched resurrection.

Pray like someone who knows the Healer personally.

Love like someone who has been held by mercy.

And never, ever forget this truth:

You are **UNSHAKABLE**

Your Commissioning

This is not the end of your story. This is the beginning of your assignment.

The songs God sang over your brokenness were never meant to stay private. They're meant to become public declarations that shake the kingdom of darkness.

Your midnight is someone else's morning. Your survival story is their hope strategy. Your healing testimony is their healing weapon.

Stop waiting for permission to step into what God has already commissioned.

Rise with the authority of someone who has touched Heaven in hell.

Speak with the confidence of someone who knows God's voice in the dark.

Move with the boldness of someone whose scars have become credentials.

You are not just healed. You are deployed.

You are not just restored. You are commissioned.

You are not just surviving. You are thriving with purpose.

You are **UNSHAKABLE.**

Now go make someone else unshakable too.

The journey doesn't end here. It multiplies through you.

Acknowledgments

My Unshakable Circle

To God, my Healer and Redeemer:

Thank you for transforming my near-death experience into a story of resurrection. Every breath I take is a testament to Your faithfulness and love.

To My Dearest Princess And My Sister: You carried me, prayed, believed, and stood firm when the reports said otherwise. Your unwavering love held me together, and you are my greatest blessing.

To My Spiritual Army: Thank you to the ministries of Curry Blake, Create Church pastors and elders, and Rev. Joe Egbe (Good News Ministries Int'l UK), whose worldwide chorus of faith lifted me from death's door and strengthened my spirit.

To My Lifelines: My deepest gratitude to Dr. Araj and the hospital team for their skilled hands and compassionate hearts, and to Mary (ARMI) and Cora, whose wisdom and concern truly saved my life.

To Jill, Diana Lookabough, My WHOZ Sisters, And All The Countless Souls Across The globe:

Your collective faith and support created a powerful shield. This miracle is a reflection of the love and strength you poured into me.

Your names are written in my heart and recorded in Heaven.

The Scroll of Testimony

Apostolic Mentors
- Curry Blake – John G. Lake Ministries
- Pastor Jerry Eze – NSPPD
- Apostle Joshua Selman – Koinonia
- Apostle Tim Atunnise Founder, GLOVIM Bible College & Seminary
- Apostle Niyi Aniyah – Waterbrooks
- Daniel Kolenda – Christ for all Nations
- Rev. Joe Ighe – Good Nws Wrn Outreach
- Pastors Joe & Sia Omega Fire Ministries UK
- Dr. Godswill Moses
- Evangelist Onyemobi Oguazi Breath ovt Power
- May & Brent Shein ARMI Anniag Wommack Ministry
- Rich & Dorothy Van Winkle The Shepherd's House, Lewisville

GOZ/WHOZ
- Apostle Diana Lookabough, Leader
- Keith Pierce
- Renee Henry
- Robin Vincent
- Fran – placed the gold mantle

Global Ministries:
- ARMI – Andrew Wommack Ministries
- Faith Tabernacle Church Ota, Nigeria
- Creflo Dollar Ministries
- Bill Winston Ministries
- Kenneth Copeland Ministries
- Create Church

Healing Hands
- Dr. Araj & UT Southwestern Medical Team
- Pastor Rich Van Winkle – treul gave BRS interbed
- Debbie Viggs – suggested grounding for swollen feet

THE AUTHOR OF LIFE
Abba Father, Jesus

CATHERINE OGIE

GOZ/WHOZ
Apostle Diana Lookabough
- Keith Pierce
- Renee Henry
- Robin Vincent
- Fran
  - Placed the gold mantle Voujsed by the

GOZ/WHOZ
- Apostle Diana Lookabough, Leader
- Keith Pierce
- Renee Henry
- Robin Vincent
- Fran – placed the gold mantle

Enterprising Women
- Jill Hellwig – Brand New U Coaching
- Tebra Kolath
- Patti Covington
- Sandy Palisch
- Malika Roberts
- Esther Chung
- Debbie Ford

The Inner Circle of Faith
- Princess
- Family
- Leaders & Colleagues at Work

RESURRECTION GALLERY

When God Rewrites the Ending

Celebrating life, heritage, and the faithfulness of God. From 15% to 100%—a living testimony.

A Prophetic Word to You, Dear Reader

These photographs are not merely documentation of physical healing—they are prophetic declarations over your own life. When doctors gave me a death sentence, I could not have imagined these moments. But God. These two words changed everything, and they can change everything for you too. As you look at my before and after, I pray you see a preview of your own resurrection. Whatever death sentence you're facing, God specializes in rewriting endings.

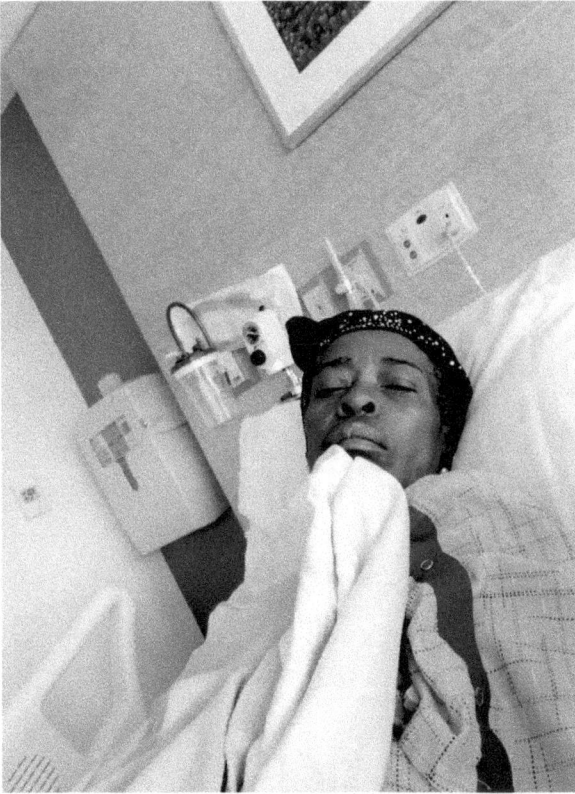

PHOTO 1: THE BEGINNING October 15, 2022 | Emergency Room

The night I discovered I'd been walking with a silent heart attack. Frail, afraid, but not forsaken. This is where my resurrection story began.

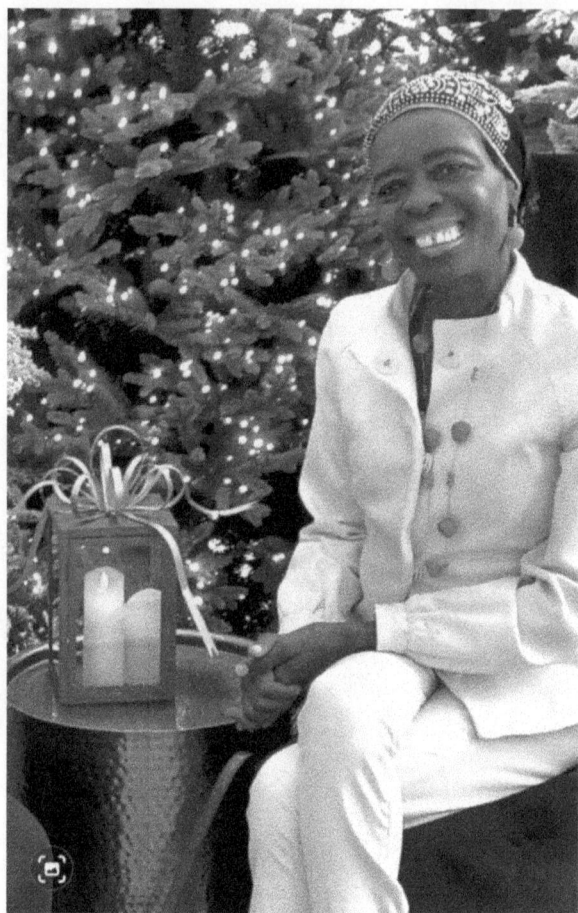

PHOTO 2: HOLDING ON TO HOPE Christmas 2023

While others celebrated, I was fighting for my life. The smile you see was defiance—my declaration that even in suffering, I would choose God's promises over my circumstances.

PHOTO 3: RESURRECTION SUNDAY Easter 2024

By Easter weekend, I stood in the choir for all three services—singing, worshiping, dancing. The same lungs that once struggled to breathe were now lifting praises to the King of Kings. This is what victory looks like.

PHOTO 4: RADIANT RECOVERY 2024

From hospital beds to outdoor joy. The same body that could barely walk is now thriving. When Heaven speaks life, death has no choice but to obey.

PHOTO 5: THE CELEBRATION OF LIFE 2025

Standing in front of "LIFE" was prophetic. After being given a 15% chance of survival, God gave me 100% victory. This was not just survival—this was resurrection power on full display.

PHOTO - MANTLED-2025

Seated on a throne, crowned in victory. This is not arrogance—this is the declaration that I am a daughter of the Most High King. What was meant to destroy me became my coronation. I am unshakable.

The throne represents the authority God restored. The crown represents the glory He placed upon my healing journey. This is what it looks like when God rewrites your ending.

"Thus far the Lord has helped me." —1 Samuel 7:12

Your Resurrection is Coming

Whatever you're facing right now, whatever death sentence has been pronounced over your life, God is not done with you. Your story is not over. Your resurrection is coming.

The same God who brought me from the hospital bed to the throne is ready to bring you from your valley to your victory. Hold on. Keep believing. Keep declaring. Keep fighting.

Your "after" photos are coming. Your testimony is being written.

Be **UNSHAKABLE.**

PRACTICAL TIPS FOR YOUR HEALING JOURNEY

These practical insights were born from real battles, real valleys, and real victories. They are not just wellness tips—they are weapons of survival, born from faith, tested in fire, and sealed with breakthrough. May they help you walk boldly toward your own healing.

Prioritize Rest Like Your Life Depends on It—Because It Does

Healing doesn't happen in a hustle. In your weakest moments, your body is crying for restoration. Honor that cry.

🕯 **UNSHAKABLE Wisdom:** Rest is not a weakness; it's a weapon.

Clean Up Your Diet—Your Gut is Talking

What you eat can either feed inflammation or fight it. Eliminate highly processed foods, added sugars, gluten (if sensitive), dairy (if sensitive), and nightshades (if you are experiencing inflammation). Keep it clean. Keep it natural.

🪨 **Tip:** opt for organic, whole foods. Hydrate with purpose.

Get Outside—Touch the Earth That God Made

Sunlight, fresh air, and grounding (such as walking barefoot on grass) may sound simple, but they're profoundly healing. Nature testifies to God's goodness. Let it restore your soul and regulate your hormones.

🌿 **UNSHAKABLE Insight:** Creation is not just scenery—it's therapy.

Turn Down The Volume of Fear—Turn Up The Voice of Truth

Detox from constant bad news. Flood your mind with Healing Scriptures, worship, and testimonies. Set the spiritual atmosphere in your home and body.

🎧 **Tip: Play Healing Scriptures day and night.** Faith comes by hearing.

Stay in Community—Isolation Is The Enemy's Playground

Let people pray for you. Let them sit with you. Let them remind you who you are when you forget.

💭 **UNSHAKABLE Reminder:** God often sends healing through the hands of others.

Advocate For Yourself (You Know Your Body Best)

Doctors are helpers, not gods. Ask questions. Read every label. Challenge what doesn't sit right in your spirit.

📖 **Empowered Living: Learn.** Research. Pray. Repeat.

Don't Ignore Your Mental Health

Consider seeking the guidance of a counselor, coach, or prayer partner. Process the trauma. Allow yourself to grieve, forgive, and reframe your thoughts.

💬 **UNSHAKABLE Truth:** Your soul needs healing, too.

Move—Even If It's Just An Inch At A Time by setting small, achievable goals like stretching or short walks. Celebrate each step forward, knowing that consistent movement supports physical and spiritual renewal, building confidence in your healing process.

Don't despise the day of small beginnings. On your weakest days, a walk to the mailbox is a win. On your stronger days, take the stairs. Celebrate progress, not perfection.

🏃 **Tip: Movement is medicine.** Track your wins. They matter.

Speak Life—Even When You Feel Death

Words create atmosphere. Prophesy your healing. Declare the promises of God as if your life depends on it—because it does.

📣 **Daily Declaration:** "I shall not die, but live, and declare the works of the Lord." (Psalm 118:17)

Recognize The Spiritual Battle—and Fight Accordingly

Wear your armor. Pray in the Spirit. Fast when prompted. Anoint your space with oil.

♡ **UNSHAKABLE Armor:** You are more than a patient—you are a warrior.

Celebrate Every Win (No Matter How Small)

The day you eat without nausea. The night you sleep through without pain. Stop and give thanks. Gratitude accelerates healing.

🌿 **Healing Hack:** Journaling progress builds momentum and faith.

Stay Expectant (Even When You're Still Waiting)

If He promised healing, He will complete it. Expectancy is not naïve; it's prophetic.

💧 **UNSHAKABLE Hope:** You are not waiting for anything. You're waiting for glory.

HEALING RESOURCES

Your journey doesn't end here. These resources are not just tools; they are your continued arsenal for victory,

Medical Support Network

Premier Medical Centers

UT Southwestern Medical Center - Dallas, TX

Mayo Clinic - Rochester, MN

Cleveland Clinic - Cleveland, OH

Baylor Scott & White Heart Hospital - Plano, TX

Prescription Cost Relief

GoodRx - www.goodrx.com (Up to 80% savings)

Mark Cuban Cost Plus Drugs - www.costplusdrugs.com

Walgreens Prescription Savings Club

CVS ExtraCare Pharmacy Rewards

Nutritional Resources

Blood Sugar Monitoring

Freestyle Libre CGM (Continuous Glucose Monitoring)

Dexcom CGM (Real-time blood sugar tracking)

Faith-Based Nutrition Experts

Dr. Don Colbert - Divine Health (www.drcolbert.com)

Dr. Steven Gundry - Gundry MD (www.gundrymd.com)

Jordan Rubin - Garden of Life Products
(www.gardenoflife.com)

Mental Health & Spiritual Coaching

Professional Support

Light University - (www.lightuniversity.com)

Better Help - www.betterhelp.com (24/7 counseling access)

National Alliance on Mental Illness (NAMI) - www.nami.org

Crisis Support

National Suicide Prevention Lifeline: 988

Crisis Text Line: Text HOME to 741741

Continued Spiritual Growth

Recommended Reading

Divine Health by Don Colbert, MD

Healing Prayer by Barbara Shlemon

Jesus Calling by Sarah Young

The Circle Maker by Mark Batterson

Worship & Declarations Playlists

Search "Healing Scriptures" on Spotify/Apple Music

Download the Bible App (YouVersion) for daily healing verses

APPENDIX A

DAILY DECLARATION

Daily Declarations for Healing

These declarations are drawn from the Unshakable journey and rooted in Scripture. Speak them aloud over your life, your health, and your circumstances, personalizing them to your specific needs. Let faith rise as you decree what God has already declared.

Morning Declarations

I Declare Life Over Death

"I shall not die, but live, and declare the works of the Lord." (Psalm 118:17)

This is not where my story ends. God still writes my chapters. I am alive by divine decree, sustained by resurrection power, and walking in victory. No weapon formed against me shall prosper. I am unshakable and confident in God's sovereignty.

I Declare Divine Health

"By His stripes, I am healed." (Isaiah 53:5)

I receive divine health in every cell, every organ, every system of my body. I reject sickness, disease, and infirmity. My body is the temple of the Holy Spirit, and it operates in divine order. I am whole, I am well, I am healed.

I Declare God's Presence

"The Lord is my shepherd; I shall not want." (Psalm 23:1)

I am not alone in this battle. God walks with me through every valley, every hospital room, every moment of fear. His presence is my peace. His voice is my comfort. I will fear no evil, for He is with me.

Evening Declarations

I Declare Rest and Restoration

"He gives His beloved sleep." (Psalm 127:2)

I lay down in peace and sleep soundly, knowing that God watches over me. My body is restored as I rest. My mind is renewed. My spirit is refreshed. I wake up stronger, healthier, and more alive than before.

I Declare Victory Over Fear

"God has not given me a spirit of fear, but of power, love, and a sound mind." (2 Timothy 1:7)

I silence every voice of fear, doubt, and anxiety. I reject the lies of the enemy. I stand firm in faith, knowing that God is faithful. I am courageous. I am confident. I am unshakable.

Appendix B

Prayers for Divine Healing

Prayer For Divine Healing

Father God,

I come before You as Your beloved child, in need of Your healing touch. You are Jehovah Rapha, the God who heals. You are El Shaddai, the Almighty. You are the Great Physician, and nothing is impossible for You.

I ask for complete healing in my body. Restore what has been damaged. Renew what has been weakened. Resurrect what the enemy tried to kill. Let Your healing power flow through every cell, every organ, every system.

I receive Your healing by faith. I declare that I am healed, whole, and restored. I will live and not die. I will declare Your works. I will testify to Your goodness.

In Jesus' mighty name, Amen.

Prayer For Strength In Weakness

Lord Jesus,

I am weak, but You are strong. I am tired, but You are my sustainer. I am overwhelmed, but You are my peace.

When I cannot stand, hold me up. When I cannot speak, speak for me. When I cannot see the way forward, be my light.

I lean on You, Lord. I trust in Your strength, not my own. I rest in Your promises, not my circumstances. I believe that Your grace is sufficient, and Your power is made perfect in my weakness.

Thank You for carrying me when I cannot walk. Thank You for breathing life into me when I am gasping for air. Thank You for being my ever-present help in times of trouble.

In Jesus' name, Amen.

Prayer for Peace in the Storm

Abba Father,

The storm is raging, and I am afraid. But I know that You are with me. You are the God who calms the seas and silences the winds. You are the God who walks on water and commands the waves to be still.

Speak peace over my mind. Speak peace over my body. Speak peace over my circumstances. Let Your perfect peace, which surpasses all understanding, guard my heart and mind in Christ Jesus.

I will not be shaken. I will not be moved. I am anchored in You. You are my refuge, my fortress, my strong tower. I run to You, and I am safe.

Thank You for being my peace in the storm.

In Jesus' name, Amen.

SCRIPTURE ARSENAL FOR SPIRITUAL WARFARE

These scriptures are your weapons. Speak them aloud, write them on your walls, and meditate on them day and night. Let the Word of God be your sword, shield, and source of victory, empowering you in spiritual warfare.

Healing Scriptures

"But He was wounded for our transgressions, He was bruised for our iniquities; the chastisement for our peace was upon Him, and by His stripes we are healed." (Isaiah 53:5)

"Heal me, O Lord, and I shall be healed; save me, and I shall be saved, for You are my praise." (Jeremiah 17:14)

"Beloved, I pray that you may prosper in all things and be in health, just as your soul prospers." (3 John 1:2)

"He sent His word and healed them, and delivered them from their destructions." (Psalm 107:20)

"I will restore health to you and heal you of your wounds, says the Lord." (Jeremiah 30:17)

Victory Scriptures:

"I shall not die, but live, and declare the works of the Lord." (Psalm 118:17)

"No weapon formed against you shall prosper, and every tongue which rises against you in judgment you shall condemn." (Isaiah 54:17)

"But thanks be to God, who gives us the victory through our Lord Jesus Christ." (1 Corinthians 15:57)

"Yet in all these things we are more than conquerors through Him who loved us." (Romans 8:37)

"The Lord will fight for you, and you shall hold your peace." (Exodus 14:14)

Faith Scriptures:

"Now faith is the substance of things hoped for, the evidence of things not seen." (Hebrews 11:1)

"Jesus said to him, 'If you can believe, all things are possible to him who believes.'" (Mark 9:23)

"So, then faith comes by hearing, and hearing by the word of God." (Romans 10:17)

"For we walk by faith, not by sight." (2 Corinthians 5:7)

"And whatever things you ask in prayer, believing, you will receive." (Matthew 21:22)

THE WEAPONS OF WARFARE

Drawn from Chapter 3 of Unshakable, these are the spiritual weapons that secured victory in Catherine's battle. Use them in your own fight.

Weapon 1: The Word Of God

The Word is your sword. Speak it aloud. Declare it over your body. Write it on your walls. Let it saturate your mind and spirit.

"For the word of God is living and powerful, and sharper than any two-edged sword." (Hebrews 4:12)

Weapon 2: Worship

Worship shifts the atmosphere. It silences fear. It invites the presence of God. When you cannot pray, worship. When you cannot speak, sing.

"But You are holy, enthroned in the praises of Israel." (Psalm 22:3)

Weapon 3: Prayer And Intercession

Prayer is your direct line to Heaven. Persistent, fervent, faith-filled prayer moves mountains and changes outcomes.

"The effective, fervent prayer of a righteous man avails much." (James 5:16)

Weapon 4: Anointing Oil

Anointing with oil is a biblical act of faith. It symbolizes the presence and power of the Holy Spirit.

"Is anyone among you sick? Let him call for the elders of the church, and let them pray over him, anointing him with oil in the name of the Lord." (James 5:14)

Weapon 5: Forgiveness

Unforgiveness is a poison that blocks healing. Forgiveness releases you from bondage and opens the door for miracles.

"And whenever you stand praying, if you have anything against anyone, forgive him, that your Father in heaven may also forgive you your trespasses." (Mark 11:25)

Weapon 6: Testimony

Your testimony is a weapon. It silences the enemy. It encourages the weary. It glorifies God.

"And they overcame him by the blood of the Lamb and by the word of their testimony." (Revelation 12:11)

Weapon 7: Unity—A Global Army Of Faith

A global army of faith acts as a powerful shield of collective spiritual energy, courageously absorbing doubt and fear as we stand united in strength and prayer.

"How good and pleasant it is when God's people live together in unity." (Psalm 133:1)

Weapon 8: The Blood Of Jesus—The Ultimate Weapon

There is no force more powerful than the Blood. It not only covers sin—it heals sickness, silences accusation, and destroys demonic assignments.

"And they overcame him by the blood of the Lamb..." (Revelation 12:11)

14-DAY UNSHAKABLE HEALING DECLARATIONS

Speak these truths over your life every morning. Let these declarations be a source of daily encouragement, uplifting your spirit and strengthening your faith

Week One: Foundation of Faith

DAY 1 - IDENTITY DECLARATION

"I am fearfully and wonderfully made. Every cell in my body was designed by God for health and wholeness. I reject every diagnosis that contradicts God's Word over my life."

Scripture Focus: Psalm 139:14

DAY 2 - DIVINE HEALING

"By His stripes I am healed. What Jesus accomplished on the cross is my inheritance today. I receive divine healing into every organ, every system, every function of my body."

Scripture Focus: Isaiah 53:5, 1 Peter 2:24

DAY 3 - SUPERNATURAL STRENGTH

"The same Spirit that raised Christ from the dead lives in me and gives life to my mortal body. I am strengthened with might by His Spirit in my inner man."

Scripture Focus: Romans 8:11, Ephesians 3:16

DAY 4 - PEACE OVER ANXIETY

"I cast all my anxiety on Him because He cares for me. The peace of God, which surpasses understanding, guards my heart and mind in Christ Jesus."

Scripture Focus: 1 Peter 5:7, Philippians 4:7

DAY 5 - RENEWED MIND

"I am being transformed by the renewing of my mind. I think on things that are true, noble, right, pure, lovely, and admirable. My thoughts align with heaven."

Scripture Focus: Romans 12:2, Philippians 4:8

DAY 6 - VICTORIOUS LIVING

"I am more than a conqueror through Christ who loves me. No weapon formed against me shall prosper. Every valley in my life is being lifted up."

Scripture Focus: Romans 8:37, Isaiah 54:17

DAY 7 - DIVINE RESTORATION

"God restores my soul. He leads me beside still waters. Even though I walk through the valley, I will fear no evil, for He is with me."

Scripture Focus: Psalm 23:1-4

DAY 8 - SUPERNATURAL FAVOR

"I have favor with God and man. Divine appointments are arranged for my healing. The right doctors, treatments, and breakthroughs are coming to me now."

Scripture Focus: Proverbs 3:4

DAY 9 - FINANCIAL PROVISION

"My God supplies all my needs according to His riches in glory. Every medical bill, every treatment cost is covered by His abundant provision."

Scripture Focus: Philippians 4:19

DAY 10 - FAMILY HEALING

"As for me and my house, we will serve the Lord. The healing that flows through me extends to my children, my spouse, and my household."

Scripture Focus: Joshua 24:15

DAY 11 - TESTIMONY POWER

"I shall not die but live and declare the works of the Lord. My testimony will bring healing to others. My story is a weapon against despair."

Scripture Focus: Psalm 118:17

DAY 12 - SUPERNATURAL ENERGY

"Those who hope in the Lord will renew their strength. They will soar on wings like eagles; they will run and not grow weary."

Scripture Focus: Isaiah 40:31

DAY 13 - DIVINE PROTECTION

"No plague shall come near my dwelling. He has given His angels charge over me to keep me in all my ways. I am hidden in the secret place of the Most High."

Scripture Focus: Psalm 91:10-11

DAY 14 - UNSHAKABLE FAITH

"I am unshakable because my foundation is built on the Rock. My faith does not waver. I believe God's report above every other report."

Scripture Focus: Matthew 7:24-25

Bonus: Emergency Declarations

When Fear Attacks: "God has not given me a spirit of fear, but of power, love, and sound mind" (2 Timothy 1:7)

During Medical Procedures: "The Lord is my light and my salvation; whom shall I fear?" (Psalm 27:1)

In Waiting Rooms: "Those who wait on the Lord shall renew their strength" (Isaiah 40:31)

During Pain: "This momentary, light affliction is working for me an eternal weight of glory" (2 Corinthians 4:17)

Remember: These declarations are not just words—they are weapons. Speak them with authority. Believe them with your whole heart. Watch God move on your behalf.

"Death and life are in the power of the tongue, and those who love it will eat its fruit." (Proverbs 18:21)

A FINAL WORD FROM CATHERINE

The book you just read is more than ink on pages. It's a prophetic invitation.

An invitation to believe again.

An invitation to fight back.

An invitation to become unshakable.

The same God who gave Catherine a new heart is ready to give you a new chapter.

Don't wait for permission. Don't wait for perfect conditions.

Don't wait until you "feel ready."

The land of the living is calling your name.

Rise. Speak. Declare. Live.

You are seen.

You are loved.

You are **UNSHAKABLE.**

CONNECT WITH CATHERINE

YOUR HEALING JOURNEY DOESN'T END HERE

You've read the story. Now become part of the community.

Whether you're walking through your own valley, standing in the gap for someone you love, or simply need a reminder that miracles still happen—**you're not alone**. Join thousands who are choosing faith over fear, declaring healing over their circumstances, and living unshakable lives.

STAY CONNECTED

Website: www.newheartpublishing.com

Email: hello@newheartpublishing.com

Social Media: Facebook: @CatherineNewheartpublishing Instagram: @catherine.newheartpublishing YouTube: Catherine NewHeartPublishing

Share Your Testimony: Use **#UnshakableHealing** to inspire others with your breakthrough story

WANT MORE?

📖 **Order Additional Copies** UNSHAKABLE is available at Amazon, Barnes & Noble, and major retailers *Perfect for friends, family, book clubs, and church groups*

🎙 **Join the Podcast** *Unshakable with Catherine Ogie* — Coming Spring 2026 Real stories. Honest conversations. Divine breakthroughs.

📷 **Join Our Healing Community** Receive weekly encouragements, healing scriptures, prayer support, and exclusive resources Sign up at www.newheartpublishing.com

✍ **Submit a Prayer Request** We believe in the power of united prayer. Let us stand with you. Email: hello@newheartpublishing.com

📚 **Invite Catherine to Speak** Available for churches, conferences, women's gatherings, and healing services Booking inquiries: hello@newheartpublishing.com

---

YOUR STORY MATTERS

If this book has impacted you, we'd love to hear about it. Your testimony could be the lifeline someone else needs today.

Leave a review on Amazon or share your story with #UnshakableHealing

---

Remember: Your diagnosis is not your destiny. God's report is the final word.

You are seen. You are loved. You are UNSHAKABLE.

ABOUT THE AUTHOR

Catherine Ogie is a board-certified mental health coach, ordained minister, and founder of NewHeart Publishing. She is a recipient of the U.S. Presidential Lifetime Achievement Award, recognizing more than 25 years of service to vulnerable and underserved communities.

Over the last 25 years, Catherine has worked across the nonprofit, coaching, and consulting worlds—supporting adults and youth facing mental health challenges, crisis, and major life transitions. Her work focuses on helping people rebuild their lives with dignity, stability, and hope. She is also a contributing writer to the Healthy Futures blog, where she sparks conversations about trauma, resilience, and whole-person wellness.

After a near-fatal diagnosis of catastrophic heart failure and a 15% chance of survival, Catherine experienced a medically documented 100% recovery that reshaped her life and message. Her journey of resilience invites others to let hope and trust in God rewrite their story.

Today, she equips high-performing leaders to trade the shame of their past for the strategy of their future, helping them reclaim strength, purpose, and unshakeable faith.

Catherine is a member of ARMI (Association of Related Ministries International) through Andrew Womack Ministries, a Woman House Leader, and affiliated with Kingdom Harvest Alliance and Glory of Zion.

She lives in Dallas, Texas.

COMPANION &
UPCOMING BOOKS

Unshakable Faith: 30 Days of Divine Healing Declarations

Daily devotional for chronic illness, spiritual warfare, and supernatural recovery

From Broken to Blessed: A Woman's Guide to Healing After Trauma

Christian self-help for overcoming pain, finding purpose, and reclaiming joy

The Prophetic Prayer Warrior: Activating Your Authority in Spiritual Warfare

Intercessory prayer strategies, spiritual warfare tactics, and breakthrough testimonies

Heart Failure to Heart Whole: A Medical Miracle Testimony

Inspirational true story of surviving congestive heart failure through faith and medicine

Unshakable Workbook: 12 Weeks to Breakthrough Healing

Interactive Bible study, prayer journal, and healing action plan for women in crisis

www.ingramcontent.com/pod-product-compliance
Lightning Source LLC
Chambersburg PA
CBHW022020090426
42739CB00006BA/219